MW00331130

BECOMING BLACK

Personal Ramblings on Racial Identification, Racism, and Popular Culture

David F. Walker

Portland, Oregon

Drapetomedia

Becoming Black:
Personal Ramblings on Racial Identification, Racism, and Popular Culture

by David F. Walker

Published by
Drapetomedia, LLC
Portland, OR 97213
www.drapetomedia.com
www.BadAzzMoFo.com
Printed in the United States of America
First Edition
November 2013

Library of Congress Control Number:
2013954463
ISBN-13: 978-0-9833557-9-3
ISBN-10: 0983355797

Dedicated to the memory of Joe Walker, Amanda Walker, Catherine Brown Walker, Washington Brown, Mary Brown, Catharine Mulatto Brown, Mary Ann Settle, Mary Henry, Shadrick Banks, Thomas Banks, Mary Banks, James Nelson Hancock, Lelia Moore, Laura Vaughters Hancock, William Henry Vaughters, Mary Jane Vaughters, Sam Venable, Samuel Venable, Katy Venable, Nannie Jackson, Isaac Jackson, and Susan Brown, who were more than property, they were my family.

A special dedication to my grandparents, Marshall and Nannie Walker, who showed me how to hold on to the humanity that others would deny me.

About the Cover

Much consideration went into the image that would be used for the cover of this collection of essays. In the end, I decided on a stylized graphic of Bert Williams. Any discussion surrounding the intersection of racial ideology and popular culture in America is, by default, a conversation about Bert Williams—even though most people don't realize it. Sadly, the collective illiteracy and historical amnesia that grips this country by the throat on a daily basis—threatening to choke the life out of all of us—includes the dumbfounded stares of complete ignorance when you ask most people if they've heard of Williams.

Egbert Austin Williams was born in the Bahamas in 1876. By the end of the 19th century, Williams was one of the most popular vaudeville performers in America, having partnered with George Walker in 1893. As the comedic duo of Walker and Williams, they played throughout the United States and Europe to sold-out audiences, performing such hit plays as *The Sons of Ham* and *In Dahomy*. Although it may seem strange, both men performed in blackface, even though they were both Black, and billed themselves as "Two Real Coons." Black performers appearing in blackface was a common practice in those days, and both Walker and Williams were just two of many entertainers whose careers were dictated by the trappings of racial ideology set and enforced by White people. Walker and Williams helped pave the way for other Black entertainers, and along with a group of other stage performers, founded The Frogs, a fraternal organization for Black entertainers and professionals. The duo broke up in 1907, after Walker became ill, passing away four years later at the age of 38. Williams's career flourished after the duo broke up, but sadly, he also died young, passing away in 1922 at the age of 46.

During the height of his career, Williams was one of the most popular entertainers in the world. At the same time, he was a Black man living in America, subject to the racism and oppression that defined the Black experience in America. In *Nobody: The Story of*

Bert Williams was one of many Black vaudeville performers who donned black-face as part of their routine. On the left is Williams as he looked out of make-up, and on the right is him in character. In many ways, Williams symbolizes the Black experience in America—an existence of duality between reality and the constructs of racial ideology.

Bert Williams, Ann Charters (1970) quotes legendary comedian W.C. Fields as having described Williams "as the funniest man I ever saw and the saddest man I ever knew." Mel Watkins (1994) elaborates, "Much of that sadness derived from Williams's inability to adjust to the bias and consequent humiliations he faced as a black man in America despite his stature as an entertainer."

Although he is not well remembered—nor are his contributions to the world of entertainment—Bert Williams remains an important figure in both the world of racial ideology and popular culture. With his face blackend by burnt cork, and his adopted stage persona, Bert Williams was a Black man pretending to be a Black man. He stands as a symbol of what so many Black people in America are—the accepted personas and mannerisms of what it means to be Black, acted upon in our daily lives, then reflected back to us in popular culture and entertainment, all the while we're something far more complex underneath. And as this collection of essays tries to make sense of what it means to be Black, and how Black as a racial identifier came to be in conjunction with popular culture, it is altogether fitting and appropriate that an image of Bert Williams grace the cover of this book. To be clear, using Bert Williams is not meant to be in any way disparaging to the man, rather it is a way of representing what so many people of color have had to do in their day to day lives.

Table of Contents

Introduction

I dropped out of college for what I was sure would be the last time in the summer of 1989. My first of several forays into the world of higher education began with me studying graphic design and illustration, and the grand dream of being a comic book artist. By 1989, however, my interests had shifted, I had become disillusioned by the world of academia and, perhaps most important, I was convinced, at the ripe age of twenty, that there was nothing school could teach me. Thus began my adventures in the real world.

My problem with school was not that I didn't want to learn; it was that I didn't want to learn what was being taught. I never believed that I knew everything there was to know, just that I could learn more outside of the restrictive confines of school. As it turns out, I wasn't that far off base. After dropping out of college, I embarked on a journey of experiential learning. Libraries and bookstores became my favorite places, getting my hands dirty doing things, and engaging in conversations on any number of subjects became my favorite activities. I studied history, literature, and film. Over the course of twenty years, I started my own publication, produced and directed movies, became a professional writer, and worked as a newspaper editor, all of which were done without any sort of formal education in those fields. Everything I learned, I learned by reading, doing, and talking to other people.

In the summer of 2010, for a variety of reasons, I decided to go back to college and finish what I abandoned more than two decades earlier. The most difficult part of being back in school was "proving what you know" through academic citation. Time and time again, I seemed to butt heads with instructors, who demanded I back up what I knew with some quote or some citation from a source beyond my own experience. I would then spend hours—and days—culling through academic journals trying to find proof that I knew what I knew. Part of me understands the need to do this, but part of me can't help but feel disdain for the process. Much of my time in college felt like I was drowning, while my instructors would ask, "How do you know you're drowning?"

"Because I can't swim, I'm in water over my head, and there's nothing for me to hold on to!" I would respond.

And then my instructors would respond, "Without academic proof supporting your theory that you are drowning, your assertion cannot be proven valid. You must show what drowning is, if you want to prove you are drowning."

Don't get me wrong, because not all of my instructors were like that. Some respected the model of experiential learning, and helped me make connections to academic theories that supported what I had learned through life in the real world. In fact, these same supportive instructors were the ones that introduced me to the concept of experiential learning, which before returning to college was what I called "stuff I learned from doing things." So you see, if nothing else, college can help you expand your lexicon and the vernacular used to express or define yourself.

All of this has been a long-winded way of building up to the introduction of this collection of essays—a preface, if you will, that wasn't quite preface material, so it is part of the introduction.

What you are about to read (at least I hope you're about to read) is a collection of essays built around racial identification and the intersection of popular culture, written as part of my senior project for school. The main focus of these essays is the evolution of racial identification in America, primarily as it relates to Blacks (or African Americans, if you prefer), and how this identification works in conjunction with mass media, mostly through a cinematic frame of reference. These essays are far more personal and auto-biographical than they are academic. That position may not sit well with some people, and that's fine.

The choice to go down a route that favors the personal over the academic springs from my personal belief that impressing instructors is not nearly as important as sharing information and wisdom with others, especially those who have yet to make the discoveries you've made. We should, all of us, be teachers and students at any given moment—sometimes the exact same moment. As a film critic, and later as a filmmaker and author, my goal has been to make myself understood by as many people as possible. I don't want to be boring (as I probably am with this introduction), nor do I want to rely on an overabundance of words that forces the reader to consult a dictionary. Perhaps most important of all, I wrote these essays this way because I'm not an academic. I'm a guy who watches, listens, and reads, thinks about it all, and then writes something down, period.

There are, throughout most of these essays, a limited number of citations.

3

This is my feeble attempt to give my work some semblance of academic credibility. There are far fewer citations to be found in this collection of essays than there are sources listed in the bibliography. The reason there are so many sources listed in the bibliography is because as an experiential learner, I wanted to try and give some credit to the books that have steered me along on my way. There are no direct references to Howard Zinn's *A People's History of the United States* or *Slow Fade to Black* by Thomas Cripps in these essays, but both had a tremendous impact on me, which I think is evident in how I write and think. To that end, the bibliography is as much a recommended reading list as it is a list of direct references, and most of the works listed I read long before returning to college. Yes, I actually read Paulo Freire's *Pedagogy of the Oppressed*, just because.

The essays in this collection all deal with race and racism (and I would suggest reading them in order—but that's just me), and draw from my own personal experiences and thoughts. Everything I have written deals with the racial identification of Blacks in America, in part, because that is the racial identification that was assigned me in my youth, and that I continue to use today. Even though I'm writing about the Black experience in America, everyone reading this work needs to know that I know that the oppression of African Americans is not something exclusive. Other people of varying shades, gender, beliefs, and backgrounds have endured unfathomable oppression in this nation, and my not mentioning them at every given opportunity is not a dismissal of all they have experienced. I acknowledge the injustice, oppression, and suffering of all people. I honor the sacrifices of all who have sought to regain the humanity that has been stripped of them, and humbly thank you all for the lessons that your experiences have taught me. In fact, I hope that someone reading these essays will be inspired to do their own research, and to write about their own thoughts and experiences, just as I was inspired by people like James Baldwin and Malcolm X (not that I'm comparing my nonsensical ramblings to them).

In closing, I'd like to share a quote from Frederick Douglass: "Knowledge makes a man unfit to be a slave." Now, I know some may take offense at Douglass's use of androcentricism, but let's look past that for a moment, and really think about this. *Knowledge makes human beings unfit to be enslaved.* What this means is that liberation from oppression comes from the acquisition of knowledge. But it is not just the oppressed that must be taught and set free, it is the oppressor as well. We live in a world of ideological constructs of inferiority and superiority that leads to the oppressed and the oppressors, but our fates are tied together. We must educate others and ourselves, otherwise we will all continue to be enslaved in one way or another. Ultimately, that is what I'm trying to say with this collection of essays. My work as a writer and storyteller is not just for Black people, or the oppressed, because enlightenment is not something that should be exclusive. If the light of wisdom, equality, and tolerance is not shone on all people, then the darkness of ignorance, injustice, and hatred threatens everyone.

Jim Brown in the 1968 film *Dark of the Sun*. Brown prematurely left a successful career in football to pursue a career in Hollywood, and in the process became one of the first Black heroes in film. He was crucial in changing the way Black masculinity was portrayed in film and television, which by default helped change the way Black men were viewed in society.

Jim Brown and the Question

"If you're smarter than me, tell me some shit. I'll listen, you know. This is an open forum." – Jim Brown

It was a little after one in the afternoon on Monday, August 5, 1996, and the heat in Los Angeles felt brutal. Sweat flowed from every pore of my body, soaking my clothes with perspiration, but it wasn't the heat making me uncomfortable. It wasn't the heat filling me with dread, making me want to run and hide like a scared child. No, my discomfort came from the man sitting across from me, staring with an intense gaze that filled me with fear. Jim Brown sat silently, and if I didn't know better, I would have thought he had some kind of special x-ray vision that allowed him to see through my skin and muscle—and even my bones—right into my soul. At that point in my life, Jim Brown was, without a doubt, the most intimidating person I had ever met. Nearly twenty years later, I still have yet to meet anyone as imposing and intense.

At the height of his career as a running back for the Cleveland Browns, Jim Brown was considered the greatest football player in the game. Brown played for Cleveland from 1957 to 1965, setting records, breaking records, and earning the sort of reputation few human beings ever earn. He retired from football prematurely, choosing instead to pursue a career in acting. But rather than hindering the legend surrounding him—tarnishing the god-like glow that comes from scoring 100 touchdowns in 93 games—Brown's early retirement made him that much more impressive. He had, after all, left the game on his own terms, looking down upon the world from high atop Mt. Jim—a lofty peak that no one else had ever scaled—and from that vantage point, Brown saw the next mountain he would climb.

By and large, the world can be divided into two different types of people. The first type is the person who hears the name Jim Brown and thinks "greatest professional football player of all time." The second is the type who hears the name Jim Brown and thinks "action hero." Of course, there are those that think of both, as well as a select few that think of Brown's impressive, but lesser-known college career in lacrosse, but for the most part, Jim Brown's name evokes specific perceptions dependent on specific interests. For me, an out-of-shape kid weaned on too much television, too many movies, and not enough sports, Brown was first and foremost a movie star. Football was that thing he did before he became an action hero in films like *The Dirty Dozen* and *Slaughter*.

After leaving the NFL in 1965, Brown made a seamless transition to Hollywood. He made his first film appearance in 1964's *Rio Conchos*, while he was still playing for Cleveland. When production delays during the filming of *The Dirty Dozen* caused him to miss training camp, Art Modell, owner of the Cleveland Browns, threatened to fine Brown for every week he missed. Instead of missing more weeks, Brown simply retired early, and went on to become a movie star. He wasn't the first Black leading man in mainstream Hollywood, nor was he the first Black action hero in the movies, but he was the first Black actor to be both a leading man and an action hero. Before Brown, lead roles went almost exclusively to Sidney Poitier, and supporting action hero roles went to Woody Strode. Other actors like Harry Belafonte, Ivan Dixon, and James Edwards had moments here or there, either as leading men, or as action heroes, but none had ever really been both.

It was Brown's role in Hollywood that placed him at the top of my list of people to interview for a documentary I planned to produce. For many years, I had grown increasingly interested in the so-called blaxploitation movies of the 1970s, those larger-than-life actions films that starred actors like Brown in movies with such attention-grabbing titles as *Slaughter's Big Rip-Off* and *Three the Hard Way*. Growing up in the 1970s, I saw relatively few of these movies in the theater, but I knew of them from the articles I would see in *Ebony* and *Jet* magazine. My family, like many Black families, had subscriptions to both. When you went to visit family and friends, issues of *Ebony* and *Jet* sat on the coffee table. In the smoke-filled barbershop where you got your hair cut by guys named Cletus and Sonny Boy, there were issues of *Ebony* and *Jet*. Anywhere you found Black people, you found issues of *Ebony* and *Jet*—glossy publications, one over-sized, the other digest-sized, that proudly proclaimed, "There's some Black folks here." And it was through the pages of these periodicals I first became introduced to the world of Black popular culture, and blaxploitation films.

I wouldn't get to see most of these films until the home video revolution of the 1980s and 1990s made it possible for me to view the movies that had been etched into my imagination since childhood. I knew who Pam Grier was, but didn't get to see her in action until I finally rented *Foxy Brown* on

VHS nearly fifteen years after its theatrical release. Through the miracle of home video, I had the opportunity to watch the blaxploitation movies that had captured my childhood imagination. The exploration of a genre that rose up through the dull din of throwaway B-movies, shone like a brilliant star for a brief time, and then seemed to disappear into obscurity, came at a time when I found myself stumbling along a path of personal understanding clouded by racial identification. In other words, I started to delve deep into the world of blaxploitation at the same time I was trying to figure out what I was doing with my life, and, equally as important, trying to figure out where I fit in as a Black man in America. At the time, I was in my twenties, and incapable of realizing that it was all tied together—my interest in blaxploitation, searching for a purpose in life, and trying to understand what it meant to be Black. In his own way, Jim Brown made it all come crashing together.

I knew going into our meeting that Brown had a reputation for being able to strike fear into the hearts of lesser men. On his comedy album *Wanted: Live in Concert*, Richard Pryor described Brown in a way that was as profane as it was profound. It is one thing to hear Pryor joke about how menacing Brown can be, but to be in the presence of Brown is something else altogether. It is the difference between someone telling you about an earthquake and actually experiencing one. In fact, it's no wonder Pryor compares Brown to the seismic shift of tectonic plates. "He come over to the house, and if you ain't up, you think it's an earthquake," Pryor joked on his album.

But it's not just the comedic observations of Richard Pryor that had served as a warning. For months, as I doggedly pursued Brown for an interview, others tried to prepare me for what awaited. I needed to interview Brown for my documentary, and with every contact I made with someone that knew him, with every conversation where his name came up, there also came the warnings, as if Jim Brown were more than a man.

"Jim will ask you questions there are no answers to, and how he deals with you will depend on how you answer the questions," Shelia Frazier, co-star of *Super Fly* and *Three the Hard Way* told me.

Max Julien, the iconic actor best known for his starring role in *The Mack* warned: "If you get Jim mad, he won't hesitate to kick your ass."

To hear others talk about him, Brown was an unwritten law of physics—the one capable of changing the very nature of being through either intellect or physical force, depending on his mood. These warnings sounded almost silly—like unbelievable folktales of Paul Bunyan or John Henry—but like all legends, the legends of Jim Brown had some basis in truth. Having dealt with him on the phone before meeting him in person, I felt prepared for my encounter. You see, even on the telephone, Brown is intimidating. Before sitting down face-to-face, when I would call on a regular basis, requesting an interview, the conversations were short and to the point, with Brown seldom saying more than five words—"hello," "not now," and "call later." The important thing to keep in mind was that he never came out and said "no," and he always told me to call back some other time. After five or six exchanges like this, I suspected that Brown was testing my resolve—that he would never consent to an interview, unless I proved myself worthy of his time. I called him once again, and he shot me down, once again. But before he could say, "Call later," and hang up, I said: "Look, Jim, I know I'm being a pest, but I'm not going to stop calling until you give me the interview, so we can keep playing this game, or we can just get it over with." There was a brief pause on the other end of the line—a pause most people wouldn't have noticed unless they'd had a half dozen conversations with Brown, in which there had been no pauses. And so, after the pause that lasted no more than one or two seconds, Jim gave me a date, a time, an address, and hung up the phone.

My interview with Brown was part of a second wave of conversations with Black actors and filmmakers that had been integral players in Hollywood during the blaxploitation era. I had already interviewed more than a dozen people, and as I drove up the winding road to Brown's house in the Hollywood Hills, I felt a sense of confidence. That confidence was quickly shattered when an attack dog forced me to scurry up on to the roof of the car. Brown's maid, an aging Mexican woman, dragged the dog off, explaining in

**On August 5, 1996, Jim Brown asked me, "What is black?"
The question changed my life.**

a heavy accent that I didn't need to be embarrassed, because this happened all the time. Meanwhile, as I climbed down off the roof of the car, I could see Brown inside his house, holding court with a group of men that looked to be part of the Nation of Islam. They all watched me, and I wished that at least one of them would laugh, as opposed to the collective indifference they all seemed to regard me with.

I waited by the car until the bow-tied Muslims left, and Brown motioned for me to come into his home. We shook hands, his hand engulfing mine the way my grandfather's did when I was a child, and in that act alone, Jim Brown turned me into a little kid. The attack dog, the ambivalence of the stone-faced NOI, and the massive grip of Jim Brown were the precursors to what was to come—an afternoon that would stay with me the rest of my life.

As my camera operator set up the lights and the camera, and I wired Jim for sound, I went into my standard explanation of the documentary. "Basically, this is going to be about the Black films of the 1970s," I said. Back then, I seldom used the term blaxploitation before an interview, as many people took it to be something negative. One actress nearly kicked me out of her house for using it, so I had learned to avoid using it in initial conversations.

Before I could finish my explanation of the documentary, Brown cut me off. "I'll do this interview, but only if you can answer one question for me," he said. "What is Black?"

"African American," I said.

"No," Jim Brown said. "What is Black?"

"I'm talking about the films that were produced in the 1970s, and marketed towards a predominantly Black audience," I said.

"I know what you're talking about," said Brown. "But you haven't answered my question. What is Black?"

"Black is a racial designation, for people of African descent. It is a term used to identify people by their physical attributes."

"No. What is Black?"

By this point, I had started to sweat. I'd been warned: "He'll ask you questions there are no answers to, and how he deals with you will depend on how you answer the questions." Was this one of those questions? Was there no answer to this question?

"Black is a term often used to describe an inner-city existence as it relates to people of African descent. Music and movies marketed to this demographic, to the people that live in these neighborhoods, is what we call Black, because it's supposed to appeal to people with dark skin—Black people," I said.

Jim stared at me, saying nothing. His eyes tore through me as I realized I had no idea what Black was. I had struggled most of my life to understand what it meant to be Black, and even found a meaning that seemed to work for me, but when all was said and done, I didn't really know anything.

"What is Black?" Jim Brown asked again. The tone in his voice said that his patience was wearing thin.

I paused for a moment, taking a deep breath. "Jim, I don't know the answer to your question. I can tell you what I think Black is, and I've done that, and none of those answers is what you wanted to hear. So, either I don't understand the question, or I don't have the answer you're looking for. Either way, I can't answer you in a way that's going to satisfy you. All I can do is my best to make myself understood, and hope that if there is a misunderstanding between us, you will ask me to clarify my meaning."

Jim Brown nodded his head and, I think, he smiled. "Start recording," he said.

Twenty minutes later, the interview was over. In the years that have followed, I have not seen or talked to Jim Brown. But his question has stuck with me, echoing in my mind, attaching itself to my consciousness in a way that at times makes it inseparable from who I am. I have become the question, the question has become my life, and to this day, it is something I struggle to answer: "What is Black?"

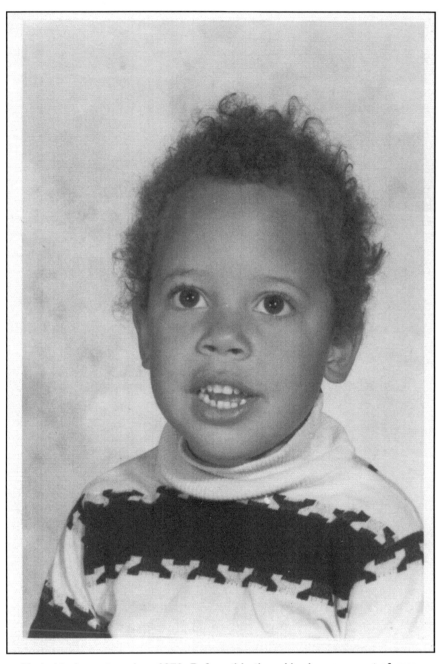

Me in kindergarten circa 1973. Before this time, I had no concept of race or racial identification. I was still just a kid. All of that quickly changed, and I soon became Black, my identity defined by the physical differences between myself and the other kids at school.

How I Became Black

"It goes a long way back, some twenty years. All my life I had been looking for something, and everywhere I turned someone tried to tell me what it was...I was looking for myself and asking everyone except myself questions which I, and only I could answer." – Ralph Ellison

On June 12, 1967, the U.S. Supreme Court handed down their decision in the case of Loving vs. Virginia. Richard and Mildred Loving had each been sentenced to a year in prison for violating Virginia's laws regarding interracial sex and marriage. Richard was White, Mildred was Black, and before the Supreme Court ruling that over-turned standing laws regarding interracial relationships, their marriage had been illegal in seventeen states. The ruling in Loving vs. Virginia was a landmark decision and a decisive victory in the struggle for civil rights, making interracial relationships legal and, in time, helping to remove the crushing stigma of alienation and racial ambiguity that often befell the children conceived by parents of different races. Eighteen months after the ruling in Loving vs. Virginia, however, bi-racial children were still outcasts in a society that preferred to think of race in terms of Black and White. This is the America that I was born into.

For me, race has always been a difficult concept to wrap my brain around. In the most simple of terms of racial identification, my mother was White and my father was Black. Nowadays—thanks largely to

Loving vs. Virginia—this is much more commonplace, so much so that we call the children born of interracial relationships bi-racial, or multi-racial, or in some cases, we don't call them anything at all. But when I was a child, and "race mixing" was not nearly as acceptable as it is now, you didn't have the luxury of being bi-racial. When you were around White kids they called you a white nigger, while the Black kids called you a Black honkey—but that was only when they wanted to be mean. When the kids were just being kids, then they would innocently call me things like zebra or Oreo cookie. Either way, I was never made to feel like I belonged in any world—too White for Black kids and too Black for Whites—and as far back as I could remember I felt something that I would only be able to explain when my vocabulary had expanded enough to include the word "alienation."

Despite the alienation—despite the fact neither team wanted me on their side—time and time again I was either asked to identify myself racially, or I had racial identification hefted upon me. For a child of any racial or ethnic background, the weight of identification can be crushing. It is like being handed a giant trunk that is too heavy to carry with your arms, so instead it is placed on your shoulders, where it threatens to snap your spine. This trunk is filled with all the things associated with race (or religion, or gender, or class, or sexuality)—all the assumptions, stereotypes, and accepted realities attached to whatever it is you are identified as being—and it weighs more than anything you will ever carry. It will make you as much as it will break you. And like many children, I was made to carry this trunk at a very young age, with no warning of what was about to be placed on my narrow shoulders.

Before going any further, it is important to define in some capacity the meaning of race—specifically race in America. This is a definition I will return to from time to time for elaboration and greater clarity, but for the time being, now is as good a time as any to define race. Dr. Joy DeGruy (2005) defines race as follows:

> Despite our constant everyday use of the term 'race' and our reference to various races, the biology of human beings is such that there are no real differences between human beings. Race is frequently characterized by skin color, hair texture, facial features, etc. These differences are offered as examples of how we differ as humans. The underlying assumption is that there is a genetic/biological component to these distinctions that defines the 'races.' (p. 21).

I can recall a time when I had no concept of race. Yes, I was aware of the physical differences within the world and within my family—some people had dark skin, while others had light skin—but race, or more specifically, what we in this country associate as being race, was a foreign concept to me. I didn't become aware of race until I was four or five years old. I had just started kindergarten, and it was here that I was first asked a question that has now been asked me more times than I can remember: "What are you?"

At the time, I didn't understand the question. I knew who and what I was in the world I had come from—a world that consisted of being raised by my mother, who was White, and my grandparents, who were Black. The world that I had lived in was kind and nurturing, and I was accepted without anyone ever asking me, "What are you?" The thing I quickly learned, however, was that there was another world outside the one I lived in. In this other world,

Black people and White people didn't live in the same house. In this other world, no one had a Black grandmother dropping them off at school, and a White mother picking them up after school. And in this other world I quickly learned that I didn't belong to either side of a divide that I had never seen before. This divide was an invisible line, with the White kids on one side, and the Black kids on the other.

Perhaps it is because of the assumption of innocence American society places on children, but there is a high degree of denial on the part of adults when it comes to how they believe children perceive race. This is, of course, merely an extension of the persistent societal and cultural denials surrounding race, and by extension, racism. In the book *The First R: How Children Learn Race and Racism*, authors Debra Van Ausdale and Joe R. Feagin (2001) point out that "White adults abdicate their responsibility to recognize and combat racism when they deny that race and racism can even exist in serious forms among young children" (p. 3). Issues of race and racism do, in fact, exist among children, because these issues exist throughout American society. It is impossible for children not to be impacted by race and racism, because as Van Ausdale and Feagin point out, "[children] are surrounded with racial imagery, thinking, discourse, and behavior. They observe it, experience it, and absorb it in different places and from the people they encounter. It is ubiquitous" (p. 200).

In an ideal world, adults seek to protect children from the dangers that threaten their safety. Some of these dangers are easier than others to address, and so most children know the importance of wearing a seat belt, or not playing with fire, as these are very real concerns related to safety and well-being. But when it comes to protecting children from the emotional, intellectual, and psychological dangers of racial identification, most adults are ill-prepared—even the most loving and caring adults. As a result, young children venture out into the world, stepping into kindergarten classrooms for the first time, or onto playgrounds, only to have entered into a world that has already set them up to be either the oppressor or the oppressed. And in an instant, a child can be transformed into something other than what they had once been. This instant is when race, gender, or other identifiers become not just a seemingly innocent tool of recognition, but a role that has been assigned. Little girls become more than just their parents' daughters, they become the societal assumptions of what girls and women are thought to be. Children who can be defined by the concepts of race cease to be children, and begin the long, painful journey of becoming what they have been racially identified as being.

Some people may not recall the moment of their transformation—the moment they started becoming aware of the differences that forcibly define us. Personally, I recall when my transformation began, when my perception of myself collided with the perception of others, and I first started becoming Black. It was clear from looking at me that I was not White—my skin was darker, my hair was curlier. At the same time, I didn't look much like the other Black kids. Still, I looked more like them than I did the White kids, and so it was decided, by the kids in my kindergarten class that if I was anything other than a zebra or an Oreo cookie, I was Black.

I suspect that if there had been more Black kids at my predominantly White school they may have protested my being placed on their team. It was clear they didn't want me, but their rejection was never as obvious—especially compared to the rejection of other Blacks that I would experience later in life. Perhaps the handful of Black kids at my elementary school figured it was just easier to let me be one of them—to recognize the futility of saying, "We don't want him either, he ain't one of us"—than it was to put up a fight. Maybe they felt the need to bolster their numbers. Or maybe they just felt sorry for me, knowing that as much as they had been made to feel like they didn't belong, I had it worse. Whatever the reasons may have been, I was not uniformly rejected by the Black kids the way I had been by the White kids, and as a result, I first became Black when I was in kindergarten. I was given a trunk to carry, and sent off into a world that identified me by the large, cumbersome crate that threatened to crush me under its oppressive weight.

Four decades later, I still struggle with the trunk that is racial identification, but I have learned how to put it down from time to time. I have learned how to remove some of the contents that can make these trunks of identification so heavy—whether they are used for race, gender, sexuality, or any other label that can be used to identify and, by default, oppress. Perhaps most important, I have learned how to open the trunk and examine the contents in an effort to be better understand who I am as seen through the eyes of others. In one way or another, I had been trying to open the trunk for years, to better understand what was inside and why it always seemed so heavy, but it wasn't until Jim Brown had asked me the question, "What is Black?" that I really decided to explore what was inside. It had been my inability to answer Brown's question—or even fully comprehend the complexity of any possible answer—that would change my life in a way on par with the transformation that had made me Black in the first place.

Starting from the time I became Black, I tried to understand what it meant to be Black. This is no easy task, as many Black people can tell you (as can others who reside in other oppressed groups), because when all is said and done, much of the racial identification of being Black has nothing to do with the actual physical characteristics associated with being of African descent. To understand the development and evolution of racial identification, it is crucial to understand the relationship created by the intersection of socio-political ideology and mass media, as well as examine the overlap of history and mass media as represented through various forms of popular entertainment, which have culminated in perceptions of race. In other words, how we as a society have come to define race in America has been determined by ideological constructs filtered through the mass media of popular culture—film, literature, television, music, etc. Popular culture is rife with racial, gender, and ethnic identifiers, but these identifiers are artificial constructs that more often than not dehumanize the group being indentified, and transforms the individual into a member of the subjugated group.

Growing up, the example of what Black people were supposed to be came from two primary sources. First, there was my family, the people I interacted with on a daily basis. Growing up in small, close-knit Black community in an otherwise all-White town, I would also consider many of my neighbors to be part of the example of what Black people were supposed to be. I grew up in southern Connecticut, just outside of New York City, in a working-class neighborhood, where the collars were blue and everyone worked hard. It was a predominantly White town, and very financially well off, except, of course, for the small pocket of working class people who lived in the "bad part of town." No matter how rich a community is, there is always a part of town where the middle class and poor people live. There are always the working-class neighborhoods, where the blue-collar families live, and the houses are not nearly as big or

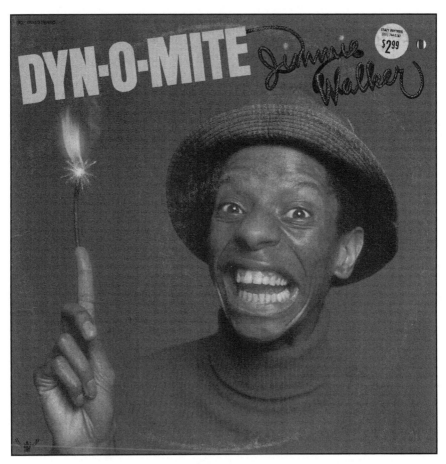

Jimmie Walker, star of the popular television series *Good Times*. The kids at school would ask me if he was my father, because we had the same last name and neither of us were White. Would you want people wondering if this guy was your father?

nice, and there's only one car in the garage, and it's older and a bit beat-up. Sometimes these households have both parents, and when they do, both of them work, and when there is only one, he or she seems to work extra hard. And the kids in these neighborhoods, no matter how hard their parents try, are never dressed as nice as the kids from the other side of town, where dad works in the city as a lawyer, and mom stays at home, sipping on cocktails in between tennis lessons.

I was one of those kids from the side of town where things weren't quite as nice. You might not get a sense that we were poor, until you saw the houses just down the street. I'm talking about the houses where the White kids got to spend the hot summers in the pool, whereas kids like me had to be content running through the sprinkler in the back yard. There weren't that many Black families in the town I grew up in, but we all knew each other because we all lived in the same neighborhood. This is where I first learned about what it meant to be Black, from my family and my neighbors. The lessons I learned were straightforward and to the point—always work hard, always say "please" and "thank you," always tell the truth, always speak properly, always address your elders accordingly as "miss" or "mister," and always remember that when you are outside in the world, you are representing your family.

The lessons I learned from my family and neighbors served me well, helping to shape me into the person I would become. More important than that, the examples set forth by my family served as a balance to other examples of what it meant to be Black—the smattering of pop culture texts that served as both banal works of entertainment and at the same time sole representations of the African American experience. The day-to-day experience of me and my family was nothing like *Good Times* or *Sanford and Son*, yet those two shows provided what amounted to the only consistent television representation of Black life in America. One took place in the tenement projects of Chicago, the other in a junkyard in Los Angeles, and though neither appeared to be anything like the reality of my family and neighbors, both served as a window into the perceived lives of African Americans.

On the side of town where I lived, we watched *Good Times*, knowing it was not what life was like—that it represented an exaggerated yet narrow vision of Black people. Meanwhile, on the other side of town, where no African Americans lived, *Good Times* became one of the few frames of reference for White people who didn't know any people of color, or whose interactions with Blacks were limited at best. From 1974 to 1976, I dreaded Wednesdays, because this was the day after *Good Times* aired—the day that all the kids came to school with some new found insights into Blackness. Tuesday nights the kids at my school would watch *Good Times*, and on Wednesday they would come to school chanting "Dyn-o-mite" and asking me if actor Jimmie Walker was my father. I marveled at how stupid they all were. I didn't watch reruns of *The Brady Bunch*, or episodes of *One Day at a Time*, and assume that these shows were representative of all White people. But then again, I knew enough White people to know that there was a vast difference between what I saw on television and what I saw in real life. The same can't be said for the White kids I grew up with. For some of them, me and the other Black kids at school were the only people of color they knew, while our family members, who cleaned their houses and did their yard work were the only Black people their parents knew.

26

The entire custodial crew at my elementary schools was made up of Black men—Mr. Brown, Mr. Lovett, and three or four others whose names I can't recall. They all lived in the same neighborhood as my family. Mr. Lovett lived across the street and three doors down, and Mr. Brown—whose first name was General—rented a room from the Hicks family, who lived next door to the Lovetts. I knew them. They knew me. And when the kids at school weren't wondering if Jimmie Walker of *Good Times* was my father—because, you know, we had the same last name—they would ask me if I was related to any one of the janitors at school. I would try to comprehend how anyone could think Mr. General Brown was my father. He was a tall, gangly man—older than my grandfather—with skin the color of dark chocolate, a perpetually pissed off look on his face, and he did not resemble anyone in my family. I assumed he always looked angry because he hated cleaning toilets and mopping up vomit. The White kids at school assumed he was my father because of the color of his skin.

When we are children, we draw conclusions based on the world we see around us in our day-to-day lives, as well as the world we see in popular culture. Throw in the lessons we are taught in school—or, equally as important, the lessons we are not taught in school—and a volatile, contradictory, unreliable formula of cognitive development begins to take shape. Our individual perceptions or race, gender, religion, and all the other labels we use to identify others and ourselves is shaped by this formula. Home environment (family and possibly neighborhood or community) + outside environment (school, work, church, etc.) + mass media (popular culture) = our perceptions. At our most basic, we are all the sum total of this equation.

We cannot change the equation itself, only the ways in which we engage each factor within the formula. That is to say, for example, that there is no getting around the fact that mass media and popular culture shapes our perceptions. However, we can change our perceptions through the way we engage and examine mass media. Our understanding of something like racial identification need not be solely informed by mass media and works of popular culture, rather it can be informed by the critical analysis and close examination of popular culture.

Who I am today is the direct result of what I recognized as a terrible imbalance in the equation of perception. From the moment I became Black, I sensed something wrong. I could not fully articulate it for many years, but what it comes down to—what I now so clearly see—is that there was no balance or alignment between my home environment and the other factors of outside environment and mass media. In my home, surround by people of color (as well as some white people), I saw with my own eyes the Black experience in America. This experience was rich with history and humanity, allowing me to see the race I had been identified as being a member of as complex collective of fully formed human beings.

By comparison, in my school lessons, the Black experience in America was relegated to a few paragraphs in vast textbooks filled with page after page of White accomplishment. To this day, I can recite the full extent of Black history I learned in school with a few short sentences. Black people were brought over from Africa as slaves. Harriet Tubman helped slaves escape through the Underground Railroad. Eli Whitney invented the cotton gin. Abraham Lincoln freed the slaves. Martin Luther King Jr. fought for equal rights. And that's it. That is the culmination of thirteen years of public education—all the lessons of Black history I learned from kindergarten to my senior year in high school. And these incomplete lessons are also the same ones taught to all the White kids who attended school with me, who only knew me and a half dozen other Black kids, and assumed we were all related to the school janitors, and that we all went home at night and sat around the dinner table exclaiming "Dyn-o-mite."

I knew at a very early age that there was more to being Black than the handful of lessons we learned in school, and the performances I saw on television. Having become Black through a combination of genetics and the perceptions of others, I grew increasingly interested in the identification I had been given. The desire to understand what I had become would lead me down a path of exploration, fueled by a desire to know as much as possible about what it means to be Black. To this day, I am still exploring—still trying to figure it all out. The most profound discovery I have made along the way—the one I try to share with everyone—is that how we define ourselves must come from within the core of our being, and not from the perceptions of others. Too many of us seek to define who we are within the context of the group, and in the process fail to define who we are as individuals.

Double Consciousness, *Roots*, and Finding Our Place in History

"After the Egyptian and Indian, the Greek and the Roman, the Teuton and Mongolian, the Negro is a sort of seventh son, born with a veil, and gifted with second-sight in this American world,—a world which yields him no true self-consciousness, but only lets him see himself through the revelation of the other world. It is a peculiar sensation, this double-consciousness, this sense of always looking at one's self through the eyes of others, the measuring of one's soul by a tape of a world that looks on in amused contempt and pity. One ever feels his twoness,—an American, a Negro; two souls, two thoughts, two unreconciled strivings; two warring ideals in one dark body, whose dogged strength alone keeps if from being torn asunder." – W.E.B. Du Bois

Part I

It is incredibly difficult in America—perhaps impossible—to be a person of color and to be thought of simply as a person. Take me for example. For the vast majority of my life, I have rarely been anywhere with other human beings, and simply been a person. Invariably, I am a Black man. That is, quite simply, how things are in America. Black people do not exist in America as people, but as people whose identity requires some sort of adjective or modifier to delineate that they are different. Think about how many times you've heard someone describe a co-worker as "a Black guy at work," as opposed to simply "a guy at work." The same is true for the Asian woman that got on the bus, or the Hispanic man standing in line at the grocery store.

There is a cultural predilection to label and identify through key descriptors tied primarily to race and ethnicity. In theory, it makes it easier to describe others this way, but in reality, it serves to transform the individual into the embodiment of the perceptions associated with the physical characteristics being identified. In other words, when someone describes the Black guy at work, the Asian woman on the bus, or the Hispanic man in line at the grocery store, they are doing more than providing a description based on physical attributes, they are, in fact, opening the door to a long list of perceptions associated with the identification of race and ethnicity. These perceptions are part of the double-consciousness that W.E.B. Du Bois wrote about.

When Jim Brown asked me, "What is Black," I struggled to answer the question. The answer to that question, as it relates to Blacks, or African Americans, or whatever term you choose to use, lies within the concept Du Bois referred to as double-consciousness. Both the term and the concept can be applied to just about anyone, and in fact, most people live within the framework of some sort of double-consciousness to one degree or another. Even though I could not answer Brown's question at the time—nor could I fully comprehend it—the fact of the matter is that I'd been looking for the answer shortly after developing double-consciousness. I began to see myself, as Du Bois describes, "through the eyes of others" at a very early age. I suspect many of us do. The moment the other kids at school began treating me differently, as if I was not as good as them, my double-consciousness began to form. It grew stronger the more they saw me as being like the Black people they saw on television, and assumed that because I shared certain physical attributes with the characters on *Good Times*, *Sanford and Son*, or *What's Happening*, that I must be like them.

Here I am—not even ten years-old—and I have been identified as something that I am not. I can see for myself what it is the kids at school think I am, because it is on television every Tuesday night, as Jimmie Walker—who is not my father—shucks and jives on *Good Times*. They think this is what Black people are like, because this is all they ever see on television of Black people—silly caricatures and hazy shadows. There is no balance to what they see. There is no depth of humanity. If you're a Black child watching this vaudevillian freak show, you are seeing yourself through the eyes of others, and you see yourself as a joke, even though you know you're not a joke. And the fires of your double-consciousness burn your soul, blister your brain, and leave you uncertain of who you are, or what you're supposed to be. This is what it's like to be Black.

Du Bois describes double consciousness as a "sense of always looking at one's self through the eyes of others, the measuring of one's soul by a tape of a world that looks on in amused contempt and pity." The eyes of others that see you, the tape that measures you, these are the ideological constructs of the dominant White race that create the perceptions of the Black race. This is where racial identification is formed, built upon the same ideological constructs that provide the foundation upon which racism is built, coming together with other key factors for the purpose of defining race. These constructs and these factors have worked to create the identifiers that provide us with the misleading answers to "What is Black." Yet these answers also lead to another question: How did Black come to be? Specifically, beyond the obvious genetic indicators witnessed through physical appearance, how did racial identification evolve in America?

The key to understanding the evolution of racial identification requires an examination of key ideological constructs through a framework that takes into consideration the confluence of factors through which the ideology has been filtered. Simply put, if you want to understand how concepts of race developed and evolved, you can't look in just one place. First, there must be the study of American history, with thorough attention paid to the phenomena of slavery, the Civil War, Reconstruction and, most importantly, how race relates to each. Second, there must be a study of mass media that includes examination of the varying types of mass media, function of the types, and the manifestation of certain types as reflections of popular culture through forms of entertainment. Third, there needs to be an examination of the intersection of mass media with historical events and facts, in order to formulate an understanding of how something like slavery or the Civil War is processed through popular culture components of mass media such as literature and film.

The television mini-series *Roots* changed the perception of slaves and slavery from something abstract to something personal. For me, it would be a defining moment in understanding who I am and where I came from.

Much of my life has been spent watching movies and TV shows, and frequently contemplating issues of race related to what I was seeing. I have also had a long-running interest in history, specifically history surrounding slavery in America. This interest was initially sparked by the television mini-series *Roots*, which for myself and millions of Americans served to recontextualize slavery as a personal experience. The problem with slavery—aside from the inherent evils of the institution itself—is that in America most people don't actually comprehend it. Slavery is more of an abstract concept, something that happened a long time ago, to people who have been dead for centuries, and it is now thankfully over. To be certain, notions of slavery do exist in the public consciousness, though these are largely inaccurate (which is something I will be covering later). Because slavery is not adequately taught in the school system, and frequently misrepresented in mass media, the magnitude of its impact is not recognized, despite the fact that even today we are living with its consequences. One of the most obvious of these consequences is the racial divide in America that exists primarily between Black and White.

Having used Dr. Joy DeGruy's explanation of race as being "frequently characterized by skin color, hair texture, facial features, etc.," I would like to elaborate more on the concept of race, delving deeper into the complexity and importance of the subject at hand. That is to say that most people don't really understand what race is all about, or what racial identification means. David R. Roediger (2008) writes:

> Though the genetic differences among groups defined as race are inconsequential, race is itself a critically important social fact; one said to be based on biology, as well as on

color, and at times on long-standing cultural practices. Race also defines the consciousness of commonality uniting those oppressed as a result of their assumed biology, perceived color, and alleged cultural, as well as the fellow feeling of those defending relative privileges derived from being part of dominant—in US history, white—race. The world got along without race for the overwhelming majority of its history. The US has never been without it. (p. xii)

In defining race, both DeGruy and Roediger strike at the heart of what is crucial in understanding racial identification in America. In theory, race is supposed to refer to a group of people with shared physical characteristics passed along genetically. Frequently, however, race is confused with culture or ethnicity, in which the physical characteristics attributed with race are combined with factors such as language, religion, geographic location, manner of dress, shared history, or any other of a myriad of identifiers, interwoven into a complex tapestry of identification. At various times in American history, different ethnic, religious, and cultural groups such as Irish, Japanese, and Jewish immigrants have all been racially identified at one point or another. But it is crucial to understand that this process is not racial identification. At best, it is a form of ethnic/cultural identification that places the individual within a larger group identity. At worse, it is an artificial construct, used to oppress both the individual and the larger group, by creating a paradigm built upon an ideological foundation of inferiority and superiority centered on cultural or ethnic characteristics and, most frequently, the seemingly obvious physical differences that make it possible to say, "You are not the same as me." This is called stereotyping. We've all done it, or have had it done to us, and we all know the power of the stereotype.

Race in America, or more accurately, the perception and understanding of race in America, is an artificial construct—the result of physical characteristics blending with ethnic/cultural identifiers, and bound together by prevailing ideology. What this means for Black people in America is that who and what we are identified as being is, to a very large extent, not based on race—it is not true or real. Instead, what passes for racial identity is in fact a mix of cultural and ethnic tropes, inexplicably tied to ideological conventions, many of which can be traced back to the days of slavery, first in the American colonies, and then in the United States. Blacks living in America, insofar as how we self-identify, or how we are racially identified by the world around us, are who we are as a result of slavery. Alvin F. Poussant (1968) writes:

> Over 300 years ago black men, women, and children were extracted from their native Africa, stripped bare both psycho-logically and physically, and placed in an alien white land. They were to occupy the most degraded of human conditions: that of a slave, a piece of property, a non-human. (p. 95)

The forced enslavement of Africans and their descendants is the fundamental truth of the Black existence in America, and crucial in understanding the evolution of what passes for racial identification. The second fundamental truth of the Black existence in America are the racial ideologies formed around the institution of slavery, intrinsically tied to works of mass media/popular culture, creating a sense a reality—backed by a biased perception of history—and furthering the mythology of racial inferiority and superiority. To explore these two fundamental truths is to embark on a perilous journey fraught with infuriating truths and heart-breaking realities; and the final destination of this journey is not a physical place, but an intellectual and emotional one—a laboratory where history becomes myth and truth gives way to ideology. It is here that our double-consciousness is born.

Part II

Based on the novel by Alex Haley, the television mini-series *Roots* first aired in January of 1977. I was eight years-old at the time, in the third grade, and not allowed to stay up past nine. My mother, in her infinite wisdom, felt that *Roots* was important enough to let me stay up past my normal bedtime. To her credit, at that time my mom already had a long history of letting me watch things that other parents might not have deemed appropriate for a child of my age. As a result of my mother's rather liberal parental discretion, my fascination with film and television was already in place by the time *Roots* aired, and my future employment in the entertainment industry was a given. I can point to four movies specifically that inspired me to go into the film business—*Planet of the Apes, One Flew Over the Cuckoo's Nest, Jesus Christ Superstar*, and *Willy Wonka and the Chocolate Factory*, all of which I'd seen before viewing *Roots*. In their own way, each of these films changed my life while I was still in my single-digits, but *Roots* had a bigger impact on me than any movie, book, or television series I had ever seen, or have since seen.

Roots aired at a time when I was struggling under the massive weight of racial identification. In school, we had already learned about slavery. It was something that was taught to us in an impersonal, abstract way that disconnected it from humanity. Black people were once slaves. Then they were set free. End of the history lesson regarding slavery. Likewise, we'd already learned about Martin Luther King Jr. at this point; this lesson consisted of my second grade teacher

37

pointing out to the class that if it wasn't for Dr. King, Tyrone Wilson—the only other Black kid in class—and I would not be allowed to go to school with White kids. These rather remedial lessons in the history of the Black experience in America summarize nearly everything I learned about the Black experience in America during my entire career in public school. Had it been left to the teachers and school districts, I may have remained adrift in an ocean of existential and historical uncertainty, trying to understand who and what I was based on inadequate lesson plans and television shows like *Good Times* and *What's Happening*. Thankfully, instead of drowning in this ocean, *Roots* provided a lifeboat, provisions, and map to lead me to dry land.

Though praised, both the novel and the television series *Roots* have also been criticized, in part for historical inaccuracies and charges of plagiarism. Criticism and plagiarism notwithstanding, what *Roots* gave the nation was a personalized narrative through which slavery could be examined. The narrative of American history is populated with names, personalities, places, and actions that recount specific stories. When school kids are taught about the Pilgrims and the Plymouth colony, they are taught about people like Myles Standish. The revolutionary War is filled with tales like Paul Revere's Midnight Run, or George Washington and his troops at Valley Forge. Slaves and slavery had no such narrative, and no such characters. In history as it is taught, slavery is something that happened to the concept of people, and not to people as individuals. It was something that happened, and it happened to people, but it did not happen to people that Americans knew or recognized. And because slavery exists as this abstract collective of a poorly defined institution populated by a group and not individuals, the slave is robbed of his

Nelson Hancock, my second-great grandfather, was born a slave in 1855.
He was the son of slave-owner John Douglas Hancock and slave Lelia Moore.
Like Nelson, many slaves were fathered by their owners. While the family tree of
John Douglas Hancock can be traced back to England in 1525, very little is
known about Lelia Moore, other than the fact that she was the property of John
Douglas Hancock. Lelia Moore was sold to another plantation before Nelson
turned five. He never knew what happened to his mother.

or her humanity. This is what slavery sought to do in its time, and what it has continued to do in much of its historical context. *Roots* gave the slave a name. *Roots* gave slavery a history filled with personal experiences. *Roots* gave the descendents of slaves—people like myself—a sense that there was more to who we'd been told we were. Therefore, despite whatever criticism can be leveled at *Roots*, nothing can change the fact that it transformed slavery from the abstract into something more tangible, and in doing so restored a bit of the humanity that had been denied Blacks.

Like many Americans who watched *Roots*, it instilled in me a curiosity about my own family history—specifically the history of my father's family—while at the same time sparking an innate interest in history that extended beyond what was being taught in school. The result is that I have spent a significant amount of time researching and documenting the history of my family, and my family's place in history. All of us are a part of history, just as our families are part of history, though most of us are seldom taught to think of things this way. A lack of personal history and illiteracy of the larger historical narrative creates a disconnect that places many people outside of the story being told. This again is a large part of the problem with how slavery is taught in the school system, which in turn is part of the problem in how many Blacks self identify, as well as the way Blacks are identified in the larger cultural context. The only way Americans can understand who they are—and by Americans, I mean all Americans, regardless of race or ethnicity—is to understand and comprehend the far-reaching impact of slavery. This is exactly what I have tried to do.

My paternal grandparents, Marshall Walker and Nannie Hancock

Laura Vaughters Hancock, my second-great grandmother, was born a slave
in 1855. Very little is known about her parents, William and Mary Vaughters,
who were also slaves. Slaves were considered property, and therefore their
lives and history as human beings were of little importance. As a result,
there are very few records of the lives of slaves other than what was used
for inventory purposes. More than a century later we are still dealing with
the dehumanization of Africans and their descendants caused by slavery.

41

Walker, were themselves the grandchildren of slaves and slave owners. Through years of research and conversations with other family members, both close and distant, I have been able to piece together a family timeline in which both slavery and immigration played critical roles. I had fantasies of tracing my family lineage all the way back to Africa, where I would discover the identity of long-forgotten ancestors. The reality is that the descendents of African slaves looking to trace their family lineage usually hit a dead end some time in the early 1800s. This is because slaves were not listed as individuals in census reports, nor were they considered human beings. Before being officially counted in the census starting in 1870, enslaved Blacks were merely listed as property on inventory manifests filed with the U.S. Census Bureau known as Slave Schedules, which listed the approximate age and the gender of the slave, but not their name. If birth records were kept, it was purely for inventory purposes, and in some cases the year of birth, if known, would go on to be recorded in the 1870 census.

Compared to the lives of slaves, the lives of White colonists and slave owners can be fairly comprehensive. There are birth records, death records, marriage records, and land ownership records to validate the existence of White people, filling out their personal history with a long list of people, places, events, and things. The slave owner existed in America as a full human being with a history, while the slave existed as property to be bought, sold, and traded, not unlike a piece of farm equipment. It is infinitely easier to trace the personal history of the slave owner than it is to trace the history of the slave, though the two are intrinsically connected in ways that many people don't understand, or want to believe. The brutal truth, however, is that if you are the descendent of slaves looking to trace your family history, sooner or later you're likely to find a rather large branch on your family tree that is a slave owner.

James Nelson Hancock was born a slave in 1855. Known as Nelson, my second great grandfather was the son of a slave owner, John Douglas Hancock (1825), who impregnated his slave Lelia Moore. John Douglas Hancock, my third great grandfather, had been married twice, both times to White women, and had at least five children between the two marriages. According to the 1850 U.S. Census Slave Schedule, John owned eight slaves, five of whom were females, but only two of whom, based on age, were likely to be Lelia. My guess is that Lelia Moore was a 14-year-old slave owned by John Hancock, which would have made her 18 or 19 when she became pregnant with Nelson. She was sold to a plantation in Tennessee sometime before 1859, as there are no slaves listed on 1860 Slave Schedule that could be her. Nelson would recall the trauma of having his mother sold to another plantation, of never seeing her again, and not knowing what happened to her. In my family, this story was passed down to his children and grandchildren, who in turn passed it on their children and grandchildren.

When I think of double-consciousness—when I think of the "measuring of one's soul by a tape of a world that looks on in amused contempt"—I think of Nelson Hancock. Here was a child whose mother was sold off as property to another plantation in another state. At the same time, Nelson's father was also his owner. Because of laws passed in Virginia in 1662, any child born of a slave mother was also a slave, and the property of the mother's owner. This law, which would eventually be passed in all slave states, reversed a previous English law that proclaimed a child's status was determined by the father. The significance in this law, as described by James Oliver Horton and Lois E. Horton (2005) is that it meant "Englishmen could increase the supply of perpetual servants and more easily maintain the racial distinction between slave and free, enslaving their own children" (p. 30). This law also made the rape of female slaves acceptable for more than two hundred years, in which millions of children were born and became the property of their fathers. This is how my second great grandfather came to exist.

Because Nelson Hancock's father, my third great grandfather, was a White man who was also his owner, it was possible for me to trace that particular branch of my family back to England in 1525. There is a long list of names, birthdates, and marriage records to validate the existence of John Douglas Hancock, making him a complete person. By comparison, I know nothing about Lelia Moore, other than her name and that she was sold off before her son's fifth birthday. History has recorded her existence as nothing more than a slave that gave birth to another slave on the Hancock plantation in Charlotte Courthouse, Virginia, and then disappeared. Where she came from, how she lived, and how she died was never considered important enough to record. She barely exists within any sort of historical narrative, and the traces of her existence that do remain have dehumanized her, rendering her as little more than an anonymous piece of furniture or a farm animal. There are millions of unrecorded and forgotten stories just like Lelia's, all belonging to the slaves whose identities barely extended beyond a listing of age and gender in property manifests.

Nelson Hancock married Laura Vaugthers, also a former slave, born in 1855. Laura was the daughter of William and Mary Vaugthers, both of whom were also slaves. Beyond their names and the years they were born, nothing is known about William and Mary Vaugthers, joining Lelia Moore as ancestors who exist as little more than forgotten property. And it would be one thing if there were only three branches of my family tree like Lelia Moore and William and Mary Vaugthers, but they are not alone. Catherine Walker, my second great grandmother, was born a slave in 1860, and her parents Washington and Mary Brown (born in 1835 and 1844, respectively), were also slaves. Washington Brown was the son of a slave named Amos Brown (1805), who in turn was both the son and property of a man also named Amos Brown (1770). Washington Brown's mother was Mary Anne Settle (1800), a slave whose owner was her father, Strother John Settle (1774). Strother Settle's family can be traced back nine generations to England in 1445. There are no records, however, of Mary Anne's mother, who had been a slave, owned by either Strother or his father William, my sixth great grandfather.

The mother of Catherine Walker was Mary Brown (not to be confused with Washington Brown's mother, Mary Anne Settle). Mary Brown (1844) was the daughter of a White man, Moses Ramey (1819), who legally married a slave named Catherine Mulatto Brown (not to be confused with her grand-daughter of the same name). Catherine's name before she was married indicates her middle and last names were likely inventory descriptions from a past property listing. There are no records to indicate who Catherine Mullato

45

Brown was, where she came from, or who her parents were. All anyone really knows about her past is that at one point she was the property of another person, possibly Moses Ramey's father, John Ramey, who owned more than twenty slaves. Members of the Ramey family came to the colonies from France in the middle 1600s. The Ramey family, who are descended from French royalty, can be traced back to my twenty-seventh great grandfather, Carlier De Remy, born in France in 1070.

Lelia Moore, Mary Anne Settle, William and Mary Vaugthers, and Catherine Mulatto Brown are four of my great grandparents who exist on my family tree with no real history to call their own. They are joined by other generations of my great grandparents Joe Walker, Amanda Walker, Thomas and Mary Banks, Samuel and Katy Venable, Issac Jackson, and Susan Brown, all of who were slaves, but whose stories have long since been forgotten. It is as if their existence didn't matter enough to be properly recorded or remembered, and their forgotten lives—like the forgotten lives of millions of other slaves—are all missing chapters in the history of this nation. On a national level, each one of these missing chapters is a part of America's history that has never been told. But on a more personal level, these chapters are pieces of your being—of your soul—that have been lost and can never be recovered, leaving you incomplete. This incompleteness, born out of a lack of history, tells you that you came from nothing, and therefore part of what you are is nothingness—you are defined by, and regarded by, a lack of understanding of what came before you. And again, this is where double-consciousness is formed.

To be the descendent of slaves is to be the heir to a fragmented history that inevitably is a frustrating mess of non-existence on one side, and, quite frequently, surprising revelations on the other side. The legacy of slavery in America is like a giant tree. On one side of the tree, massive branches extend across the Atlantic Ocean to Europe. The boughs are strong, having grown for centuries, blooming with leafs of history. On the other side of the tree, most of the branches have been chopped off and hauled away to be used as firewood. The branches that remain are short, with leafs that bloom sporadically. It is almost impossible to believe that these two drastically different sides can exist on one tree—one side lush and healthy, the other side ravaged by abuse and neglect. Yet there it is, for everyone to see, a giant tree that grows in every town and every city in America, providing shade with its giant branches on one side, while the other side, with its damaged and severed limbs that leave people wondering, "What's wrong with this tree?"

Lies of History and History of Lies: How Popular Culture Made Us Black

"The turbulent power of race is envinced by the variety of ways in which the images and historical experiences of African Americans and other people of color are symbolically figured in commercial cinema." – Ed Guerrero

In America, history is often treated as if it is some sort of tangible thing—like it is a packaged product that can be picked up off a shelf and casually examined. The most remedial study of history—American or otherwise—is not unlike walking down the cereal aisle of the grocery store, looking at the various brands of frosted flakes, sugared puffs, and toasted crunches. On these imaginary shelves of these make-believe grocery stores, there are hundreds of different brands of cereals, each one representing different aspects of history. There are boxes of Revolutionary War Flakes and further down the aisle you will find World War II Crunch, which comes in a variety of different flavors, including fruit, chocolate, and peanut butter, and along with everything from Bits of The Great Depression to Sugarcoated Western Expansion Puffs, all of these cereals are easy to identify and consume. You can pull a box of World War II Crunch off the shelf and study the label on the side, where instead of nutritional facts there are important names and dates about World War II, and this is what passes for history. But as is the case with real cereal, which contains little by way of nutritional value, this stuff offers little by way of educational value. It is, after all, impossible to package history into neatly designed products that taste good to everyone—especially young children.

The pervasive problem with Americans and history is that if the history does not come in a cleverly designed package, and it doesn't taste good, they don't want to bother with it. No one wants to eat the cereal with healthy ingredients that is not covered in sugar. It's like those old commercials for Life cereal, where the kids sit around and discuss what's inside the box. "I don't know, it's some cereal—it's supposed to be good for you. I'm not gonna try it, you try it." "I'm not gonna try it, you try it." "I'm not gonna try it. Let's get Mikey. He won't like it, he hates everything."

When it comes to history, most Americans are like those kids who don't want to try the cereal called Life (ironic, isn't it). The Mikeys of this country, who actually take nourishment from more than boxes of sugar that have been passed off as viable food sources, are sadly few and far between. The end result is a nation of the blissfully ignorant—some unintentionally so, others willfully so—who feign an understanding of the complexities of history, all gleaned from the lessons found cleverly and appealingly packaged into boxes of yummy tastiness.

In this world of palatable, easy-to-digest history, where taste is more important than fact, there is no market for a cereal about slavery. No one wants to eat Slavery Charms, even though it comes with marshmallows shaped like shackles, chains, and whips. Slavery Charms is second only to the generic brand of Native American Genocide Puffs—which tastes just like Sugarcoated Western Expansion Puffs—both of which no one wants to eat. The truth of the matter is that like the genocide of the Native Americans, there is no way to make slavery palatable. No amount of sugar, fruity flavor, or toy prizes at the bottom of the box can make the reality of slavery taste good. It is one of the worst tasting parts of American history, flavored with centuries of murder, rape, and wholesale dehumanization of people based on the color of their skin. Just opening a box of that particular cereal is enough to make most people gag with disgust; but to actually put a spoonful in your mouth and chew it, is to taste the unrelenting cruelty of slavery in America. A mouth full of used kitty litter would taste better.

The forced enslavement of Africans and their descendents is one of the most important and influential aspects of American history. Slavery and its legacy is more than a thread or two running through the fabric of this nation, it is, essentially, much of the fabric itself. It is America at its ugliest, and because

The history of slavery in the United States is like the monster in the Bugs Bunny cartoon, "Hair-Raising Hare"—America is constantly trying to give it an extreme make-over to make it seem not as bad.

slavery is so gruesome, most people would rather not look at it—they'd rather pretend that it was not as bad as some people would have us believe, or that it never really existed in the first place. And yet, there it is—staring at us like some horrific monster hiding in a closet, just waiting for the right moment to leap from the darkness and attack, mauling us with the sharp claws and pointy fangs of historical truth.

As a nation, America has grappled with how to contend with this monster. Slavery is too big to ignore or completely forget—too integral to the history and development of the country and the culture of the United States. So rather than ignore or forget this hideous monster that devoured and mauled millions of lives, it was transformed into something different. For lack of a better comparison, slavery was given an extreme makeover that recalls the classic Looney Tunes cartoon "Hair-Raising Hare." This is the one where Bugs Bunny is chased around by giant monster covered in red fur that wants to eat him. At one point, Bugs tricks the monster, attempting to file down its massive claws by giving it a manicure. In the end, Bugs Bunny manages to trick the monster once again, this time by breaking the fourth wall and pointing out the audience that is watching, which terrifies the monster forcing it to flee. In the cutest, most charming comparison possible, slavery is like that giant red monster from the Looney Tunes cartoon. First, its claws were filed down. Then it was made to believe that it should hide in fear from the true monsters—the audience.

At this point I've likely alienated some people—especially academics— by comparing slavery to breakfast cereals and the giant red monster from a Bugs Bunny cartoon (that monster, by the way, had no name in "Hair-Raising

Hare," but when it returned in later cartoons it was named Ruda and then Gossamer). These comparisons were not made to make light of slavery. No, the reason for these comparisons is, quite simply, to build a framework couched in popular culture to examine both slavery and racial identification as it is understood in America. That is to say, that what the average American knows about slavery and the concepts of racial identification, they learned from various works of popular culture such as film and television, or abbreviated and incomplete lessons in history processed to be easily understood. As a nation, more people have been educated about history through movies that are passed off as historical texts, than any sort of in-depth study. The result is a country full of people whose understanding of slavery and the Civil War comes from movies like *Gone with the Wind*, instead of anything grounded in reality.

If there are two things people don't like to discuss, it is racism and ignorance—especially when it is their own racism and ignorance. People hate looking at pictures of themselves from high school, where poor fashion choices and unfortunate hair styles threaten to identify us as being idiots incapable of making good decisions. But it is one thing to look at an old photograph and admit to having questionable taste, and something else altogether to come face to face with your own stupidity and blind racism. This brings me to *Gone with the Wind*—a national treasure of popular culture that is an instrument of racism, a cultivator of ignorance, and beloved by millions.

I first saw *Gone with the Wind* in the theater, when I was a kid in 1971. My mother took me to see all kinds of movies, but *Gone With the Wind* stands out as one of my earliest theatrical movie-going experiences. I was already addicted to television at that point in my life, but going to the movies was something almost beyond comprehension. As it was, television turned out to be a gateway drug to something far more addictive—watching films in the theater. These early childhood film-going experiences had a tremendous impact on me, and I vividly remember seeing *Gone with the Wind* and *The Wizard of Oz* during theatrical re-releases both before I was four years-old. If there is something deep inside the core of film critics that compels them to watch and study cinema differently from the average movie-watching public, then I suspect that that particular seed had been planted in me at an early age.

My love of film was apparent from the very beginning, and for reasons only she can explain, my mother allowed that interest to grow. She bought me magazines with articles about various movies before I could fully comprehend what the articles were about. Most often, I just looked at the pictures. And within the pictures that appeared in these magazines, there was inevitably behind-the-scenes photos of the production process. It was these pictures of movies being made that let me know that films were something that were constructed—that they didn't just exist as some sort of reality we watched on the big screen. This understanding, which came to me by the time I was four or five years-old, had a profound impact on me, because it meant that I never confused film with real life. I never mistook what I saw on the screen for being anything other than make-believe (although, as I will explain later, films did impact my perceptions of reality). I knew at a very early age that Oz was not a real place, and that there was no such thing as munchkins or flying monkeys. This profound perception also kept me from mistaking *Gone with the Wind* for anything that might be confused with reality. For me it was just a movie. Unfortunately, for many Americans, *Gone with the Wind* has become some sort of historical text, and with that perception, the ideological constructs of racism and ignorance of history have been firmly established in the minds of countless millions.

In all fairness, *Gone with the Wind* is not the most racist or historically inaccurate depiction of slavery, the Civil War, or Reconstruction to be found in pop culture texts. It is, however, the most enduring and popular of countless other works of revisionist entertainment, and as such, it is the one to get people the most riled up when addressing it as a work of racial and historical propaganda. In order to understand what is wrong with *Gone with the Wind*, it is important to understand how it came to exist as a work of literature and then film, and this requires an understanding of history.

The America Civil War fought between the states of the Union and the Confederacy is a defining chapter in the history of the United States. The causes of the war were complex and varied, though in the overly simplified versions of history that I was taught in my childhood—a version taught to virtually all Americans—the role of slavery in the war has been significantly reduced. If I were to sum up in a single sentence all the Civil War lessons I had been taught in my youth, it would read something like this: "The Civil War was fought when southern states seceded from the Union over state's rights." From a purely grammatical standpoint, that statement is a complete sentence, but from a historical perspective the sentence is incomplete. A more accurate summary of the war would read along these lines: "The Civil War was fought when southern states seceded from the Union over state's rights, especially the right to own slaves."

Despite the various circumstances and political complexities that led to the Civil War, it all comes down to the fact that the war between the North and South was fought over slavery. Some would argue that the main cause of the war was over the Constitutional rights of the states, but ultimately the rights that they are talking about deal with slavery. Others would argue that the primary cause of the war was economics. This argument, much like the argument of Constitutional rights, is completely correct. The missing factor in the economic cause of the war argument, however, is that slavery was, in fact, an economic issue.

Slavery exists in the minds of most Americans as an abstract concept, which makes it less soul-crushing to think about. The truth of the matter is that there is nothing abstract about slavery—it is the direct result of what happens when human life is reduced to an economic equation. Under slavery, Blacks in America were not human beings, but a labor force akin to some amalgam between a farm animal and a piece of machinery. Blacks were bought, sold, and traded as commodities—organic equipment that picked the cotton and tobacco grown in Southern plantations, which in turn created great wealth for a select group of property owners and business-men, while simultaneously contributing to the national economy. Yes, the Civil War was largely fought over economic issues, but those economics were the economics of slavery. It is crucial to understand this, as opposed to trying to separate slavery from the Civil War, or slavery from economics.

The Civil War began in 1861 after slave-owning states in the South seceded from the United States, forming the Confederacy, also known as the

Confederate States of America. The war ended in 1865 with the victory of the Union forces of the North over the Confederacy. During the war, President Abraham Lincoln issued the Emancipation Proclamation in 1863, essentially freeing all slaves. The following year, the Thirteenth Amendment was added to the Constitution, formally abolishing slavery in the United States. Immediately following the Civil War came what is known as Reconstruction. It could be argued that Reconstruction actually started during the war with the Emancipation Proclamation, a key defining moment in the transformation of the nation. Other historians feel Reconstruction did not officially begin until after the war. As with the Civil War itself, there are differing schools of thought regarding when Reconstruction began, and the purpose it served. There is, in fact, two markedly different historical accounts of Reconstruction and the Civil War—and as a result, significantly different perspectives on slavery—and it is these differences and the ideologies behind them that set the course for racial identification in America.

If in fact the average American has little to no understanding of the Civil War or slavery, their knowledge of Reconstruction is even more deficient. In the cereal aisle of American history, the brand that once represented Reconstruction has long since disappeared from the shelves. But for many years, Carpetbagger Crunch was one of the most popular of the history cereals, with no other competitive brands to be found. Carpetbagger Crunch was the only historical account of Reconstruction available in the former states of the Confederacy, as well most of the Union states. This particular cereal was covered with so much sugar and artificial fruity flavor that it was impossible to identify the real flavor. What's more, at the bottom of every box of Carpetbagger Crunch there was a toy prize—a well constructed alternate view of the Civil War and slavery that was more mythological construct than historical overview.

In the broadest, most general context possible, the purpose of Reconstruction was to rebuild the Union in the aftermath of the Civil War. Eleven states had seceded, many having been decimated during the war, while the abolition of slavery freed millions of Blacks, and with their freedom came the need to address civil rights and political power. The policies of Reconstruction were enacted to address these and other issues, but the perception of these policies was radically different between the North and the South. The particulars of Reconstruction are long and complicated—perhaps even more complicated than the causes of the Civil War itself—but in the end, much of the opposition to Reconstruction centered around the Blacks who had been freed. With policies dictated by the North, who had won the war, Reconstruction was viewed by many Southerners as an extension of a war in which they felt had victimized them. The anti-Reconstruction movement that emerged in the South threatened the reconciliation needed for the United States to heal from the war and move forward as a nation.

One of the main causes of the Civil War had been how to deal with slavery as more states were admitted to the Union. Free states of the North that did not have slavery capitulated to the slave states of the South in concession after concession, but in the end the concessions were not enough. Four years of war settled one of the main issues, but not the root cause, and as a result, Reconstruction was not reconciliation and rebuilding in the aftermath of the Civil War, but merely an extension of the conflict on to a different battlefield. At the heart and soul of the conflict surrounding

Reconstruction, as with the Civil War, were the prevailing ideologies of race. The belief in White superiority and Black inferiority were the ideological constructs upon which the justification for slavery was built. For many people, this ideology did not go away just because of the Civil War, the Emancipation Proclamation, or the ratification of the Thirteenth Amendment. And here is where we begin to see that the Civil War, Reconstruction, and slavery are all part of something much bigger—the American War of Racial Ideology.

The American War of Racial Ideology is exactly what it sounds like— a conflict at the center of which is the perception of race. On one side of the battle are those looking to destroy the myths of White superiority and Black inferiority, creating in their place an ideological construct of equality for all human beings. Both the Civil War and the abolition of slavery represent significant battle victories in the American War of Racial Ideology, but a close examination of Reconstruction and its failure reveals that the war itself was lost. Millions of Blacks were freed during the Civil War, but their status as citizens of the United States and human beings was held at bay by ideology. If slavery is the crucial defining factor in the racial identification of Blacks in America, then it is the failure of Reconstruction that allowed the prevalent ideologies to endure, which in turn leads us to *Gone with the Wind.*

Written by Margaret Mitchell and published in 1936, *Gone with the Wind* is the embodiment of the failure of Reconstruction, and the decisive victory of anti-Reconstructionists in the continued perpetuation of racial ideology. Mitchell came from a family with strong roots in Georgia that

58

favored slavery, supported the Confederacy, and were staunchly opposed to Reconstruction. Anti-Reconstructionists were not only opposed to civil rights for freed Blacks, as a culture, many Southerners saw the Confederacy as the victims in what they called the War of Northern Aggression. Within this cultural context, Reconstruction was another humiliation in the face of defeat at the hands of an oppressive regime that had destroyed their way of life while trampling over their rights. Having endured one defeat, the former Confederacy refused to concede the ideological battle represented through Reconstruction. As resistance to Reconstruction grew, it threatened to keep divided a nation that had endured a brutal war that had pitted neighbor against neighbor, until Reconstruction itself gave way to the demands of the South.

The backlash against Reconstruction found its way into the mass media and popular culture of the post-Antebellum South, emerging as an alternative perspective to the Civil War and slavery, a newly formed mythology known as the Lost Cause. The myth of the Lost Cause was the former Confederacy's way of explaining and reconciling the war, but this reconciliation did not come without exacting a major toll. Bruce Chadwick (2001) writes:

> The only way mythmakers could wash away the bitterness between North and South and bring about reunification was to erase the fundamental cause of the war and all its death and destruction—slavery. The historical writings and popular culture of the late nineteenth century began this erasure, but it was the all-powerful film medium that, in thousands of darkened movies houses across the Republic, most effectively absolved the South of any blame for slavery. (p. 14)

Within the mythology of the Lost Cause, the South was a rich, noble culture that had been attacked by the North, forcing the Confederacy to defend itself. In the Lost Cause, slaves were content with their lives, in part because slavery wasn't such a bad thing—slaves loved their masters, and their masters loved them—and because Blacks lacked the intellectual capacity to care for themselves, they required subjugation to survive. This perspective, which was shared by much of the South, absolved the Confederacy of its role in the Civil War, and reconciled slavery as a magnanimous gesture of the superior White race toward the inferior Black race.

The Birth of a Nation, directed by D.W. Griffith, was adapted from Thomas Dixon's popular novel, *The Clansman: An Historical Romance of the Ku Klux Klan*. Both the novel and the film were built around an alternative view of slavery, the Civil War, and Reconstruction, in which the KKK were heroes.

There is an old adage that says history is written by the winners, but in the case of the Civil War, it was not true. As it became increasingly clear that the nation would not come together under the auspices of Reconstruction, the need for unification and post-war healing led to increasing anti-Reconstruction concessions being granted to the former Confederacy. Chief among these concessions was the assimilation of Blacks as citizens with equal rights, which was largely abandoned to appease Southerners that subscribed to notions of racial ideology. Another main concession was the acceptance of the Lost Cause interpretation of history, which began to take root within the larger historical narrative. History had been written by the losers, and it was this history that found its way not only into the classrooms of the South, but the North as well. Equally important, this other history found it's way into the popular culture of the time, which was on the verge of undergoing a radical shift with the invention of the motion picture.

The motion picture began to emerge in the late 1880s, a little over a decade after the end of Reconstruction, and a little over twenty years after the Civil War. The Lost Cause narrative had already been incorporated into countless works of popular entertainment. One of the most notable of these works was Thomas Dixon's novel *The Clansman: An Historical Romance of the Ku Klux Klan*. Published in 1905, *The Clansman* was the second book in a trilogy written by Dixon that interpreted history from a pro-slavery, anti-Reconstruction point of view. Dixon himself was a staunch anti-Reconstructionist who, as a lecturer, author, and pastor, committed much of his life work to the revisionist history of the Lost Cause. His three books were incredibly popular, with *The Clansman* making the transition to an equally popular and well-received stage play. One of Dixon's influences in writing *The Clansman* was *A History of the American People*, written by future president Woodrow Wilson, and published in 1902. Wilson, like Dixon, came from an anti-Reconstructionist family, and having been born in 1856, grew up during the Civil War. He firmly believed the South had been victimized during the war, and that slavery had been a good thing. Accordingly, *A History of the American People* is a seminal work of the Lost Cause narrative, passed off as being historically accurate.

Vivien Leigh as Scarlett O'Hara (left) and Hattie McDaniel as Mammy in *Gone With the Wind*, based on the novel by Margaret Mitchell. *GWTW* was firmly entrenched in the Lost Cause narrative that emerged in aftermath of the Civil War. The version of the slavery, Civil War, and the South that were presented in both the book and film would be mistaken for historical accuracy, and forever helped to reinforce much of the racial ideology responsible for the multigenerational dehumanization of slaves and their descendants. Despite its critical acclaim, *Gone With the Wind* is a dangerous piece of racial propaganda.

The Clansman came to the attention of D.W. Griffith, an already well-established director in the burgeoning motion picture industry. Griffith, like Dixon, was a Southerner. Dixon had been born in 1864, a year before the Civil War ended, while Griffith had been born in 1875, two years before the end of Reconstruction. Both men were raised by families that had been loyal to the Confederacy, in an environment where the mythological Lost Cause had not yet been written, but was instead being lived in a day-to-day state of post-war denial. For countless families throughout the former Confederacy, the Lost Cause was real, it was the story passed down through the generations. Dixon and Griffith were the first generation of children of the Lost Cause, born into a culture of defeated slave-owners and national traitors looking for redemption by tailoring history to accommodate their absolution. As the sons of this failed Confederacy, Dixon and Griffith helped to provide the redemption of their fathers and grandfathers through popular entertainment.

In 1915, Griffith made the film *The Birth of a Nation*, his adaptation of *The Clansman*. In an era of silent films that rarely ran more than thirty minutes, *The Birth of a Nation* ran 190 minutes, while at the same time bringing to the screen cinematic innovations that had been seldom seen in motion pictures before. Griffith used such tricks as tracking shots, cutaways, close-ups, and intercutting between two different scenes as a means to tell his story in a more heightened and hyperbolic way. In its day, *Birth of a Nation* was considered one of the most innovative works of the burgeoning film industry, having introduced a new artistic language to motion pictures, and it is often credited as the first epic movie.

But while *The Birth of a Nation* was ushering in a new era of tricks, tropes, and conventions within the world of film, Griffith, as Dixon had done with *The Clansman*, firmly entrenched his work in the narrative of the Lost Cause. Chadwick describes *The Birth of a Nation* as "a blatantly racist film that egregiously slandered American blacks and helped to create a racial divide that would last for generations" (p. 112). Griffith's film was an unrelenting portrayal of racial ideology that held firm to the beliefs of White superiority and Black inferiority, espousing the most negative of Antebellum Southern philosophies. Set during and after the Civil War, the film depicted Blacks— many portrayed by White actors in blackface—as lazy, stupid, dangerous, and a threat to the safety of White people, while conversely portraying the Ku Klux Klan as heroes determined to save the South from the scourge of rebellious slaves, free Negroes, and insidious abolitionists from the North. Griffith's film was an affront to Black people, and as the most popular film of its day, it set a dangerous precedent for how Blacks would be depicted in motion pictures. Coming less than thirty years after the failure of Reconstruction—after the nation had forsaken the equality of Blacks in favor of appeasing the South— *The Birth of a Nation* helped entrench the racial ideology of centuries past within a powerful new medium of influence in the twentieth century.

There is little denying that the worst depictions of Blacks in film can be found in *The Birth of a Nation*, and that the film helped establish the cinematic tradition of dehumanizing Blacks as a form of entertainment. It would be a mistake, however, to suggest that the practice of cinematic dehumanization begins with Griffith and his film. *The Birth of a Nation* is the intersection of mass media and subjective historical perspective clouded by ideology, as influenced by earlier works of mass media and prevailing ideologies. The connection between Dixon,

Griffith, and Wilson illustrates the nature of systemically formed ideology that would have a profound impact on society. Ed Guerrero (1993) writes:

> This volatile combination of ideas, energies, and men of the South then generated in *Birth of a Nation* points to an underlying feature of Hollywood's inscription of slaves and slavery: The racism, stereotyping, and romantic mythology of the antebellum plantation South were well established in America's literature, the 'plantation school' of novelists and historical commentary, at the turn of the century, long before they were transfigured into screen images by Hollywood. (p. 11)

What Guerrero is getting at is what many film historians seem to miss: *The Birth of a Nation* is not the beginning of racism in popular culture, but a reflection of a large cross-section of cultural thinking itself. To think otherwise is misguided, and the result of consuming a film history that has been turned into an easy to digest cereal the same way so many other histories have been processed. Aside from the fact that *The Birth of a Nation* was based on a popular novel—which in itself had already been turned into a stage play—it was not the first film to embrace either the Lost Cause narrative of the Civil War, or the racial ideology of the Antebellum South. The truth of the matter is that Griffith's film was following in a cinematic tradition that had been firmly established practically at the outset of the motion picture industry, and was hardly the first film to portray Black people as lazy, ignorant, or criminally inclined. Comedic short films like *A Nigger in the Woodpile* (1904) used White actors in blackface, while films like *The Watermelon Patch* (1905) used Black performers to tell stories centered around the most negative and stereotypical behavior of Blacks. A series of shorts featuring a character named Rastus, which include *Rastus in Zululand, Rastus' Riotous Ride,*

How Rastus Got His Pork Chop, were steeped in negative racial stereotypes, incredibly popular with White audiences, and pre-date *The Birth of a Nation*.

Even the use of blackface—in which White performers use burnt cork, makeup or some other means to darken their faces—was not something Griffith invented, nor was it first done for films like *A Nigger in the Woodpile*. The most common connotation of minstrel shows and blackface performance is a negative depiction of Black people, primarily within a comedic context. This dates back to the 1830s, when the minstrel show as it is most commonly thought of was first born. As used in these early films, blackface was a carry-over from the popular minstrel shows of the 1800s. But even minstrels shows were predated by blackface performances of Shakespeare's *Othello*, which was first mounted on the stage in the 1600s. *The Birth of a Nation*, as well as the vast majority of other films depicting African Americans from the early era of motion pictures, embraced the same ideology of Black racial inferiority that allowed the minstrel show to thrive for the better part of a century, as well as serving as a justification for slavery for three centuries.

Just as Reconstruction had been killed off by prevailing ideologies of racial inferiority and superiority, the motion picture industry that emerged at the end of the nineteenth century renewed these ideologies in the world of modern technology. Moving into the twentieth century, film would become an ever-increasing tool in the continued perpetuation of racial ideology. It is through the cinematic arts that ideas, ideologies, dreams, morals, and experiences of the human condition are played out on the screen, helping to influence, inspire, and inform people. Robert Kolker (2005) explains that "from the late nineteenth century onward, people have turned to film as entertainment, escape, *and* education—as an affirmation of the way they live or think they ought to live their lives" (p. 1). Film is a powerful medium that can influence how people think and feel about the world, and inspire their desires for what they want out of the world. Notions of love, heroism, friendship, evil, and the meaning of life can all be part of the cinematic reality, and as a result can help shape the perception of reality.

Despite creating a perception of reality, and often being mistaken as such, film is not reality. Cinema is similar to literature in that it exists as an expression of ideas, and these expressions are influenced by the ideologies of the moment. Though film may seek to express an idea or concept based in, or inspired by the truth, a movie is not the truth, but rather a constructed reality. Kolker reminds us that film "is an artificial construct, something made in a particular way for specific purposes, and that the plot or story of a film is a function of this construction, not necessarily its first principle" (p. 3). It is impossible to create an objective or truthful representation in film, due in large part to the fact that film itself is an illusion. As an artificial construct, film creates a reality that exists only within the context of itself, even when it is a representation of something that has been labeled "real" or "true." Kolker writes:

> What we call "realistic" in film is, more often than not, only the familiar. The familiar is what we experience often, comfortably, clearly, as if it were always there. When we approve of the reality of a film, we are really affirming our comfort with it, our desire to accept what we see…We respond with a desire that things could be like this or, simply, that we might want to inhabit a world that looks and behaves like the one on the screen. (p. 6).

The acceptance of film as being either realistic, or a representation of something truthful, as Kolker suggests, is based on familiarity. The popularity and acceptance of racist movies and Lost Cause films, whether it is *A Nigger in the Woodpile* or *The Birth of a Nation*, reflects not only a comfortable familiarity with the racist ideologies from which these works grew, but an acceptance of these ideologies as well. These are works informed by ideological constructs of racial inferiority embedded deep within subjective truth. It is this subjectivity of truth that informed all the various mass media texts that presented the Lost Cause as being the truth of the Civil War, slavery as being the God-given right of White people, and the inferiority of Blacks as a justification for abject dehumanization. And it is this same subjective truth that informs *Gone with the Wind*.

Compared to *The Birth of a Nation*, *Gone with the Wind* is a tame depiction of the Lost Cause. *Gone with the Wind* has no scenes of the Ku Klux Klan riding to the rescue of hapless Whites being besieged by murderous Negroes, as does *The Birth of the Nation*. Indeed, the slaves of *Gone with the Wind* are happy with their lives of servitude, content to serve their White masters, who put up with the comical sass that all happy-go-lucky slaves use to express their lot in life. At the same time, the film and the book upon which it is based, is a by-the-numbers representation of the Lost Cause from start to finish, filtered through the 1939 lens of Hollywood. That is to say that *Gone with the Wind* is as revisionist to history and dehumanizing to Blacks as audiences of that era were willing to accept. For all of its oppressive polices towards Blacks, American had moved forward enough that the narrative of *The Birth of a Nation* was no longer completely palatable. *Gone with the Wind* is not, by any stretch of the imagination, a deviation from the narrative ideologies of *The Birth of a Nation*, it is just a watered down version, with a kinder, gentler face, presented in glorious Technicolor. Chadwick describes how

Gone with the Wind helped transform the perception of the Civil War, slavery and Reconstruction:

> *GWTW*, like other silent and sound films about the war, bolstered the four-pronged presentation of the Plantation Myth that the Old South was a special place ruined forever by history's lightning: 1) all white Southerners were rich plantation owners and, in their personal lives, well-educated, romantic cavaliers; 2) white Southerners loved their slaves and their slaves loved them and they all just wanted to be left alone; 3) the North started the war, forcing the gentlemen of the South to fight the Lost Cause for four years, to lose in the end, but lose gallantly; 4) the South was devastated by Reconstruction—imposed by the federal government—and never recovered. *Gone With the Wind*, seen by just about every American in theaters and later, on television, had the power to reinforce these myths and turn them into acceptable fact. (p. 189)

The Birth of a Nation, Gone with the Wind, and all the other pop culture works steeped in the mythology of the Lost Cause, and overflowing with the ideological constructs of racial inferiority and superiority, are part of a long-enduring relationship between historical narratives and mass media that determine racial identification. In the quest to understand "what is Black"—to grasp the complexity of the factors that add up to the equation of racial identification—there must first be the willingness to look at what is presented before you with a critical eye. These presentations encompass the lessons that we are taught in school, and the images we see in the mass media, both of which should not be taken at face value, for they do not portray any of us—regardless of race, gender, or culture—in a manner that is free of ideological bias.

When I think about the history lessons I was taught over the years, I think of a fragmented, incomplete narrative that provided me with just enough understanding of Black racial identity to leave me feeling like less than a person. When I look at many of the popular culture texts that offer presentations of Black racial identity, I see an identity defined by dehumanizing inferiority. When I stroll down that make-believe grocery store aisle of metaphorical cereals that are presented as history, I see no brands that even come close to satisfying my nutritional needs. This is, in all of its repulsive ugliness, part of the Black experience in America. And yet, none of it is the definition of who I am, nor is it the definition of any other Black person. These are merely the perceptions of who and what we are, tainted by ideological constructs that have all-too-often been mistaken for reality. Perceptions, however, can be altered through critical examination and the acquisition of knowledge. This is how the world went from being flat to being round. And in terms of racial identification, it is how I went from being more than what history and mass media told me I was, by discovering the humanity that had been denied me as a matter of course.

Why's the Brotha Gotta Die?

"Here is fruit for the crows to pluck,
For the rain to gather, for the wind to suck,
For the sun to rot, for the trees to drop,
Here is a strange and bitter crop." – Abel Meeropol

I remember watching *Planet of the Apes* on a portable black and white television with my neighbor from down the street, Keith Watkins, when it first aired on network television in 1973. It is one of the transformative moments of my youth, tied to both film and television, which laid the groundwork for the person I would become. Keith was a few years older than me, and he seemed to know things I didn't know. I sat engrossed in the film as the team of astronauts led by Charlton Heston crashed on a mysterious planet and began trekking across the desolate wasteland that would eventually take them to a civilization of talking apes. I remember thinking how cool it was that one of the astronauts was Black, and that I didn't know Black people could be astronauts. Charlton Heston and the other astronauts had just started their march across the desert, when Keith leaned over and whispered, "The Black guy is gonna get killed."

Being all of five years old, I didn't believe him. I hadn't seen enough movies to know the deal, and as a result, I was shocked when Dodge, played by character actor Jeff Burton was shot dead by gorilla soldiers. I looked at my friend with incredulous wonder and asked, "How did you know that was going to happen?"

71

What Keith Watkins said next burned into my brain in a way few other things have burned into my conscious thought, before or after. He looked at me and said, "The Black guy *always* gets killed."

I didn't say a word, and more importantly, I didn't want to believe it. Somehow, in my childish mind, I refused to accept the fact that the Black guy always got killed. This belief was reinforced by the fact that the Black guys lived in both *Conquest of the Planet of the Apes* and *Battle of the Planet of the Apes* (Hari Rhodes and Austin Stoker, respectively), which served as proof positive that Keith was wrong. But it didn't take long for me to come to the painful realization that both *Conquest* and *Battle of the Planet of the Apes* were exceptions to what I slowly began to perceive as being a rule of film.

Jeff Burton (center) in *Planet of the Apes*, the first Black character I ever witnessed getting killed in a movie. He would not be the last.

Developed during my formative years as a child, this rule was a brutal truth that many Black kids such as myself had come to believe. We believed that if there was a Black person in a movie—especially a horror, science fiction, or action movie—they would be killed. There were, of course, exceptions like *Conquest of the Planet of the Apes*, as well as those films that were made for us—blaxploitation movies with seemingly nothing but Black characters that played in theaters throughout the 1970s. But when push came to shove, the perception was that outside of a select few films, Black characters always got killed off in some brutal way that, as a child, felt like it robbed you of a little bit of your soul. The cinematic truth I grew up believing was that Black characters in film were disposable. And from this truth came the cinematic archetype of the Disposable Brotha.

You won't read about the Disposable Brotha in any film theory books. To the best of my knowledge, other than stand-up comedians and the armchair film critics that populate the Internet, no one has ever talked about this subject seriously. To be sure, lists of Disposable Brothas have been generated—there's even an entire website or two dedicated to them—and you can find some observations here and there on various message boards, but there is no serious discussion of the topic. And amongst those who do discuss this subject, there are two distinctly different camps. The group that asks, "Why's the brotha always gotta die first?" is made up of people who believe Disposable Brothas are always the first characters in a movie to get killed. The second group simply asks, "Why's the brotha gotta die?" with the understanding that the Disposable Brotha may or may not die first, but that he will die. I'm part of this latter camp, having seen enough movies to know that when the rule of the

Disposable Brotha is observed in a film, the character does not necessarily die first, and in some of the most well known examples of Black characters being killed, their deaths were not the first to occur within a given movie.

Planet of the Apes served as my introduction to the Disposable Brotha when I was five years-old. By the time I was in high school, I had seen some of the most traumatic on-screen deaths of Black characters ever witnessed. I was emotionally devastated when Duane Jones was shot to death in *Night of the Living Dead.* I was dumbstruck when Jim Kelly was beaten to death in *Enter the Dragon.* Paul Winfield being eaten by deadly cockroaches in *Damnation Alley* and Yaphet Kotto getting torn apart in *Alien* both left me sick to my stomach. The culmination of these on-screen deaths, as well as all the others I witnessed, was a bitter cynicism that continued to grow, giving way to mantra I found myself repeating over and over again—"Why's the brotha gotta die?" It has taken me decades of watching and studying film, immersing myself in the art of storytelling, and simply living life as a light-skinned Black man in America, to fully understand the cause, effect, and meaning of all the deaths of Black actors (and occasionally actresses) that have been portrayed in motion pictures. And now I am prepared to answer the question—Why's the brotha gotta die?

Ultimately, the answer to this question is tied to the ideological constructs of racial identification. To that end, this particular question—seemingly posed with tongue firmly planted in cheek—is not unlike so many other questions asked about race. And to be sure, this is a question about race. After all, as an audience we are asking specifically why the African American character seems to die so often. So, whether we want to or not, we must discuss race, and understand that the answer to this particular question requires a working understanding of both the history of the United States, as well as the American film industry. The understanding of these two subjects brings us to two of the fundamental truths of the Black experience in America. The first of these truths is the forced enslavement of Africans and their descendants, which is the key defining factor in the formation of ideological constructs that serves as racial identification in America. The second fundamental truth are the racial ideologies that emerged from slavery, filtered through biased perceptions of history and mass media, to create a mythology of racial inferiority and superiority.

The film industry essentially came into existence in 1888 when Thomas Edison and his assistant William Dickson invented the first motion picture projector, the Kinetoscope. This was just two decades after the end of the Civil War, and eleven years after the failure of Reconstruction, in which an alternate history of the Civil War and slavery was essentially written by the losers. Known as the Lost Cause, this alternate history found its way into the mass media and popular culture of the time, presenting an overly romanticized view of the Antebellum South, in which the Civil War was actually the War of Northern Aggression. Equally important, within the narrative of the Lost Cause, slaves were content in their lives, fully appreciative of their White masters who loved them as they would love developmentally disabled children or well-trained pets. The depiction of Blacks within the Lost Cause narrative was in step with the same ideologies of racial inferiority and superiority that had served as a justification for slavery; the result was the dehumanization of Blacks. (To better understand the relationship between film and the failure of Reconstruction, read my essay "Lies of History and

History of Lies: How Popular Culture Makes Us Black.")

The ideological constructs that justified slavery, contributed greatly to the Civil War, fought back against Reconstruction, and found its way into post-Antebellum popular culture, was still going strong when motion pictures came in to the equation. The apologist version of historical recording, mixed with lingering animosity surrounding the Civil War and the end of slavery came together fortuitously with the burgeoning film industry, of which Edison is rumored to have proclaimed, "Whoever controls the motion picture industry controls the most powerful medium of influence over the people."

The negative portrayal of Blacks in film is as old as cinema itself. There are hundreds of short films from the late nineteenth and early twentieth centuries that represent the convergence of racist ideologies and motion pictures. Most of these films, however, have been lost, forgotten, or merely obscured by the shadow D.W. Griffith's *The Birth of a Nation*, which went a long way to bolster the myth of White superiority, and further make real some of the most negative stereotypes that define the myth of Black inferiority. Nearly every single stereotype of Blacks portrayed in *The Birth of a Nation* exists today both in film and television. Granted, there may not be images as inflammatory as those seen in Griffith's film, but nearly one hundred years later, the mainstream media is still rife with the abject and flagrant dehumanization of Blacks. The most offensive minstrel shows of yesteryear can't hold a candle to modern day "entertainment" that continues to present Blacks in a manner informed by racial ideologies that have infected this country for centuries.

By now, some of you are wondering how all of this relates to Paul

Winfield being killed in *Damnation Alley*—not to mention his deaths in *Star Trek II: The Wrath of Khan*, *Terminator*, and *Star Trek: The Next Generation*. I admit, connecting the perception that Black characters always get killed in movies to the complex history of slavery, the Civil War, and Reconstruction may seem like an intellectual stretch. The fact of the matter is that Black characters are not always killed off in movies, but enough have been killed that it has become a recognizable convention. This convention is so recognizable that when actor Ernie Hudson showed up in the comedy *Ghostbusters*, you could hear Black people in the audience say, "He's gonna die." I know. I said it myself. And when Hudson's character lived—defying the convention many people had come to expect—it felt like a huge weight had been lifted. It was as if we had been given permission to live. That an audience could feel such elation over a fictional character not dying, speaks to how ingrained the notion of the Disposable Brotha had become in the Black community.

No two people watch a film the same, just as no two groups of people see a film the same way. Racial, cultural, gender and other differences affect and influence both the individual and group perceptions of all movies. At the time of its release, *The Birth of a Nation* was hailed by many White people as a fantastic achievement, and an incredible work of art. Black people, on the other hand, were repulsed by the unrelenting racism. *The Birth of a Nation* is just one example of the differing perceptions audiences can have of a film, as is *Ghostbusters*. For much of the White audience, *Ghostbusters* was a comedy about a group of guys who hunt ghosts and save the world from a deadly spectral army. For much of the Black audience who saw the film,

Ghostbusters was a comedy about a group of guys who hunt ghosts and save the world from a deadly spectral army, and the Black guy lives in the end. For many White people in the audience, the significance of Ernie Hudson's character Winston Zeddemore living was lost on them. And the fact that this is significant to one audience over another speaks to an underlying difference in perception, which leads us right back to ideology.

The perception that there are measurable differences between races, beyond obvious physical attributes, stems from ideology. It is here that the seeds of racism are planted and cultivated, and it is here that the world splinters into various groups, separated by identifiers used to establish superiority and inferiority. These are the secret ingredients in the historical recipe of the American Way. For despite the oft-quoted notion that all men are created equal, America was not built on the principles of equality, but rather the ideology of racial inferiority and superiority. Slavery and everything connected to it is a testimony to this ideology. A detailed and analytical study of American history reveals an enduring legacy of racial ideology that systematically robbed slaves of their humanity. One of the most revealing historical events in the dehumanization of Blacks is the Three-Fifths Compromise of 1787.

The Constitution of the United States was drafted and adopted in 1787 as the supreme law of the United States. Within this revered document, initially there was no direct mention of slavery, despite the fact that it was a hotly contested issue. The Northern states had abolished slavery—though slavery had existed in the North—and there was considerable debate if Southern states would continue to keep slaves. During the Constitutional

Convention in Philadelphia, both Georgia and South Carolina refused to join the newly formed Union if slavery was abolished in the South, which allowed the door to remain open to slavery in other states. As the Constitution was being drafted, one of the emerging issues was how to count slaves.

Slave owners in the South wanted their slaves to be counted as individuals—even though slaves were considered property, could not vote, and had no legal rights. By counting slaves as part of the population, it would allow the South to be more densely populated, giving them more representation in the House of Representatives. Higher population would give the South an upper hand in both the Electoral College and greater power in the creation of public policy. The North was opposed to counting slaves as individuals, and during the Philadelphia Convention of 1787, the Three-Fifths Compromise was created, declaring that each slave was not a whole person, but instead would be counted as three-fifths of a person. This compromise, agreed on by both the North and the South, and part of the United States Constitution, effectively declared that slaves—and therefore Blacks—were not complete human beings. The Constitution was never written with people of color in mind. Joe R. Feagin (2010) writes:

> While most Americans have thought of this document and the sociopolitical structure it created as keeping the nation together, in fact this structure was created to maintain separation and oppression at the time and for the foreseeable future. The framers reinforced and legitimated a system of racist oppression that they thought would ensure that whites, especially white men of means, would rule for centuries to come. (p. 15)

For all of its political significance, the Three-Fifths Compromise is one of the most telling examples of the status by which Black people were viewed in this country—not full and complete individuals, but rather incomplete pieces of property to be tallied up as a means of determining political power. And while no one ever wants to talk about it, the ideology that helped to create a law that stated a Black person was only three-fifths of a human being still lingers today. It is not always easy to see, but it can be found in places as odd and seemingly innocuous as film and television.

So, what does all of this have to do with the brotha getting killed in films?

The answer is simple (although somewhat disturbing): Black people originally existed in America as commodities to be bought, sold and traded, and as such, they were little more than disposable. For centuries, Black lives were not considered the same or as important as the lives of White people in as much as Black people were property. From an ideological standpoint, a slave had more in common with a farm animal than with the owner of the slave. This ideology is how children were removed from their parents and sold to other plantations, never to be seen again. This ideology is how a disobedient slave was whipped into submission, or had a foot chopped off so they couldn't run away, but could still pick cotton. And this lingering ideology, in its various permutations, has influenced how Black people are treated and depicted in popular culture. In other words, the Black guy gets killed in movies because he is not as much of a human being as a White guy—his life is not as important.

When crafting a story it is crucial to develop characters, establish conflict and define the consequences that dictate the laws of reality as they exist within the cinematic world. An audience must know that the threat of the monster is real, or that the evil bad guy is truly evil, and to that end there must be examples to drive home these points. And Black characters are very good for driving home these points. Introduced as supporting characters with enough flamboyance and charisma to make some sort of lasting impression, they are then systematically killed off, proving that the threat of death is real, while simultaneously providing the White hero with enough motivation to seek revenge. This storytelling convention is not uncommon, but it takes on a different context when it is applied to a Black character. Take for example the film *The Lord of the Rings: Fellowship of the Rings*.

There are no Black characters to be found in *The Lord of the Rings*. Amongst the population of hobbits, dwarves, elves, and humans, all are played by White actors. This in and of itself sends a message that there is no place for humans or human-like people who are Black in Middle

Sean Bean as Boromir in *The Lord of the Rings: Fellowship of the Ring*. The death of Boromir helps to establish the real dangers faced by the heroes, but because he is one of many White characters in film with no Black characters at all, his death has no racial significance. If, however, Boromir had been played by a Black actor, his death would have taken on additional meaning, steeped with the context of racial ideology.

Earth—it is a world exclusively populated by White people. The closest things to people of color in Middle Earth are the monstrous orcs, which plays into a similar ideology as the one seen in *The Birth of a Nation*, where Negro savages threaten the world of whiteness. Sean Bean co-stars in *Lord of the Rings* as Boromir, one of the nine members of the Fellowship that set off on a mission fraught with danger. Boromir is killed, which lets the audience know how high the stakes are on this adventure. His death is an emotional moment in the movie, but as a White actor in a film with an all-White cast, the death of Bean's character does not resonate the same as if Boromir were Black. His character dies in a reality where it is already accepted that Black people do not exist, and so his death is merely the death of person who lives in Middle Earth.

But let's imagine for a moment that Boromir was played by actor Colin Salmon, and that Salmon is the only Black actor in the *Lord of the Rings*. There are, no doubt, fans of *The Lord of the Rings* that would argue Boromir could never be Black, because he was the son of the Steward of Gondor, and that the ruler of this kingdom was himself White. That is not part of this discussion, and I will not waste any more time arguing the minutia of this sort. All we are doing is imagining for a moment that Boromir was played by a Black actor and not reimagining the entire racial population of Middle Earth, or the ruling family of Gondor. Got it? Good. In this alternate version of *The Lord of the Rings*, the Fellowship is made of nine members, eight of whom are White, and one, Boromir, who is Black. The death of Boromir still has a similar impact, in that it establishes what passes for heroism in Middle Earth, that death is a reality that threatens our heroes, and that as an audience we should expect no less from any of the other members of the Fellowship. At the same time, as the only Black member of the Fellowship, and perhaps the only known Black inhabitant of Middle Earth, the death of Boromir takes on a different meaning, at least within the perception of certain audience members.

Because Boromir is different from the rest of the Fellowship in terms or his racial characteristics, he stands out as being different. Forget that fact that nearly half of the Fellowship is made up of pint-sized hobbits with giant hairy feet, plus a dwarf, and an elf with pointy ears, all of them have White skin, which despite their other differences, unites them with that one shared trait. And because Boromir is different from the others in the Fellowship in a way that is understood through the perceptions of racial identification, the perception of his death is something different as well. For some White audiences, the death of Black Boromir provides the required cues to establish the realities and dangers of death, and within that demographic there are those who will not react as strongly to that death, because it is the death of a person of lesser value, as defined by the ideologies of racial superiority and inferiority. Whereas for some Black audiences, the death of Black Boromir signals that there is limited space for Blacks in Middle Earth, and their role is relegated to self-sacrifice at the service of White hobbits.

In the broad scheme of things, the character of Boromir—the White one, played by Sean Bean, not the imaginary Black one—serves the same purpose as the classic Disposable Brotha. But the death of a White character in an all-white movie does not have the same resonance as the death of a sole Black character in an otherwise all-White movie—at least for most Black audiences. For Black audiences, representation in most films is significantly limited, oftentimes to a single character in an entire movie, or no representations at all. The result of limited representation and exclusion in the world of film manifests over time into a feeling of extreme alienation, as if being told over and over again, "There is no place for you in this world." And to be clear, for decades this has been the pervasive message sent from Hollywood to the Black audience. Take a look at the top grossing films of all time, or the American Film Institute's list of Top 100 movies, and a disturbing trend of Black exclusion or limited representation emerges. Of the one hundred films on AFI's list, only one has a Black actor in a leading role, and of the top ten grossing films of all time, only one has Black characters, period. Understanding this level of exclusion is crucial to understanding the deeper significance of the Disposable Brotha.

It is difficult to pinpoint the first cinematic Disposable Brotha, and the fact of the matter is that Black characters in film have historically been treated as anonymous and disposable since the earliest days of film. The modern Disposable Brotha, however, began to emerge in the early 1960s, ironically, as the result of desegregation. Prior to the Civil Rights movement of the 1950s and 1960s, the limited number of roles for Black actors and actresses were confined to an even more limited spectrum of characters. The vast majority of these characters were holdovers from *The Birth of a Nation* book of filmmaking. Black women were stuck playing sassy mammies or jungle savages, Black men were stuck playing shiftless coons or jungle savages, and the purpose of the Black character was to provide either comedic relief or a sense of menace.

With the push for desegregation in American society, so too came a push for desegregation in film, leading to an increasing number of Blacks in supporting roles. Many of these roles were still based in the old archetypes relegated to Black actors, providing the same cinematic conventions, but there emerged within this increase of inclusion a new archetype that served an even greater purpose than those that provided laughs or potential threat. The new Black presence in film meant that there were now characters whose deaths could further propel the story.

A classic early example of the Black character's death being used to propel the story is director Stanley Kubrick's 1960 film *Spartacus*. Woody Strode co-stars as Draba, an African gladiator forced to fight to the death. When Draba refuses to kill fellow gladiator Spartacus (Kirk Douglas), and as a result of his defiance is killed, it helps to fan the flames of dissent. Draba is the character that first stands up to his Roman oppressors, setting the stage for Spartacus to lead the slave rebellion. And because Draba died after having spared Spartacus's life, it now gives Spartacus motivation to avenge the fallen African. In *Spartacus* we see all the recognizable traits of

Woody Strode in *Spartacus* represents a crucial shift in the depiction of Black characters in film, and helped usher in the Disposable Brotha.

the Disposable Brotha archetype at its best—a charismatic character that makes a memorable impression, whose death helps motivate the hero into action. The fact of the matter is that Draba could have been played by any actor, but because he was played by Strode the role takes on a racial significance.

Strode was a former football player and professional wrestler who transitioned into film in the late 1930s and early 1940s with a string of uncredited cameos. Much of Strode's early work was in films set in the jungle, including roles in several *Tarzan* movies and the *Tarzan* television series. He worked with some of the best directors in Hollywood, and though his roles were small, and his acting ability limited, Strode possessed the good looks and charisma of a movie star. Strode's performance as Draba in *Spartacus* embodies one of the two primary types of Disposable Brotha. This first type is the Disposable Brotha that rivals the charisma and heroic attributes of the main protagonist, and under different ideological circumstances could have—and perhaps should have—been the hero of the story. Despite being presented as disposable, characters like Draba were crucial in the evolution of how race was portrayed in film.

The second type of Disposable Brotha is the more servile Black character that lacks the charisma of a hero, and as a result, unlike Woody Strode in *Spartacus*, would never give the hero a run for his money. One of the best early examples of this other type of Disposable Brotha is actor John Kitzmiller. Born in the United States, Kitzmiller was stationed in Italy during World War II, participated in the nation's liberation, and eventually moved there. Most of his acting career was in Italian films, with the notable exception of a little film in 1962 called *Dr. No*—the first big screen adventure of James Bond. Kitzmiller starred as Bond's go-to-guy in Jamaica, Quarrel. Most Bond movies feature a supporting character that helps 007 and is killed in the process, providing the secret agent with further justification for revenge (even though he never seems to specifically avenge anyone who's died helping him out). To that end, Kitzmiller is more of a convention within the world of James Bond than he is within the context of Disposable Brothas, because every Bond movie must have the sidekick that is killed. But within the larger context of the Disposable Brotha, the character Quarrel represents the characters whose deaths serve as fodder to the narrative, and who are stuck within the more established racial paradigm of cinema.

Another example of this type of Disposable Brotha can be found in director Jack Hill's 1968 film *Spider Baby*, featuring legendary vaudeville performer and comedic actor Mantan Moreland. With more than one hundred film and television credits to his name, Moreland is best remembered for his recurring role as Birmingham Brown in more than a dozen Charlie Chan films. Most of the roles he played were steeped in the accepted comic stereotypes of Hollywood in the 1930s and 40s. Moreland played a small role in *Spider Baby*, much like dozens of other roles he'd played in the past, only this time around his character was killed. In terms of the film's narrative, Moreland's death helped establish the very real danger presented by the crazed family in *Spider Baby*. In a more symbolic way, the death of Moreland's unnamed character was reflective of one stereotype dying off, only to be replaced by another, the intersection of the old school cinematic racial ideologies, with the changing perceptions of

87

race in popular culture.

The emergence of the Disposable Brotha in the 1960s, and an examination of the two primary types over the course of the decade, provides a glimpse at the evolution of racial identity and ideology as filtered through the lens of popular culture. In essence, what we see when we look at the Disposable Brotha is Hollywood figuring out what to do with Black male characters. On one hand, the Disposable Brotha is the cinematic continuation of the dehumanization of Blacks on a societal level. Characters like those played by Kitzmiller and Moreland are extensions of established racial constructs that audiences had seen in one variation

Film and vaudeville veteran Mantan Moreland in director Jack Hill's 1968 film *Spider Baby*. The death of Moreland's unnamed character served as the symbolic killing of one of Hollywood's oldest stereotypes, and helped give birth to the new stereotype of the Disposable Brotha.

or another for decades. Characters like the one played by Strode, however, were the beginning of a new construct. Although still a victim of the pervasive ideologies of race, Strode's Draba emerged as a contradiction to certain aspects of the existing ideological constructs. This contradiction is seen in the emergence of the heroic Black figure, whose heroism could be measured alongside that of White protagonists. This heroism stood in stark contrast to many of the accepted traits of inferiority associated with being Black, and threatened to elevate African American characters to a level that demanded respect and admiration. It is here that an ideological conflict developed, placing the inferior being worthy only of disdain within a new construct that demanded praise. The solution to this conflict was to kill the character, resulting in the Disposable Brotha.

Woody Strode played a crucial role in transforming the perception of Black masculinity in film, helping to develop the Black action hero in main-stream cinema. Following in Strode's footsteps, and building upon what he started, Jim Brown transitioned from football star to movie star, becoming both the embodiment of the emerging Black hero and the Disposable Brotha in two films, 1967's *The Dirty Dozen*, and 1968's *Ice Station Zebra*. Brown brought with him an entire fan base, made up largely of African Americans who longed to see characters that looked like them in film. The embodiment of masculinity, Brown was perfect for taking part in a deadly mission against the Nazis in *The Dirty Dozen*. His death, as traumatic as it may have been, helped drive home the danger of the bad guys, and helped to motivate the remaining members of the Dirty Dozen in their quest to complete the mission and vanquish evil. In reality, Brown's character was just as disposable as the rest of his team, most of who were killed on the mission. Likewise, his death in *Ice*

The death of Ben (Duane Jones) at the end of *Night of the Living Dead* is considered by some to be the most traumatic of Disposable Brotha deaths in film. Technically, however, the character is not a Disposable Brotha, and instead exists as one of the first Black characters in film to be portrayed outside the traditional constructs of racial identification. In other words, Ben is simply a man, not a Black man. That makes his character revolutionary, and *Night of the Living Dead* one of the most important films in the evolution of how race is presented in motion pictures.

Station Zebra served to further establish the nefarious nature of the antagonist, and raise the stakes of the mission. But for Black audience members, starved to see heroic characters that looked like them, the death of Jim Brown in these films packed a powerful punch. At long last, we as a people were allowed to participate in the grand tradition of mainstream Hollywood heroics, and not as the lead in some separate-and-unequal race film produced for segregated audiences. Unfortunately, the price of our admission to the main event was the ultimate sacrifice—we had to die.

While Kitzmiller, Moreland, Strode, Brown, and Jeff Burton in *Planet of the Apes* were integral in establishing many of the conventions that define the Disposable Brotha archetype, the one character most closely associated with the archetype is Ben in 1968's *Night of the Living Dead*. Although it is revered as a horror film, historically speaking, director George A. Romero's zombie movie transcends the genre, standing on its own as a significant work of cinema for several reasons. Along with the movies of Jim Brown, *Night of the Living Dead* helped pave the way for the modern Black action hero that would rise up a few years later in blaxploitation films. At the same time, the tragic killing of Ben (Duane Jones) in the final moments of the film resonated with audiences—both Black and White—in a way that had never happened before. Despite the fact that *Night of the Living Dead* is about a zombie uprising, it is also one of the first films to defy the ideology of the Three-Fifths Compromise by showing a Black man as a complete human being. Ben's race is never mentioned in the film, nor does he display any characteristics associated with the racial identification of African Americans, making him a character free of any form of racial ideology within the film. In other words,

Ben is portrayed as a man, not a Black man. What's more, Ben's death does not propel the story or give a White hero added motivation to fight harder to survive; it is simply the senseless loss of a human life, making his death and *Night of the Living Dead* one of the more revolutionary moments of cinematic history.

The death of Ben in the final moments of *Night of the Living Dead* is viewed by many as the defining moment in the evolution of the Disposable Brotha. When they think of Black characters killed off in horror films, the iconic character portrayed by Jones is one of the first to come to mind, the embodiment of Black life being treated as a gimmick to propel the plot. The reality is that Ben's death is unlike most that define the Disposable Brotha—or any other disposable characters in film—and it is important to differentiate the death of Ben from so many of the other Black characters that have come to an untimely demise. The death of this particular character is more in line with the cinematic trend of the era, which often saw the film's heroes gunned down in the end. *Bonnie & Clyde, Easy Rider,* and *The Wild Bunch* are all movies that ended with the deaths of the main characters. Ben has more in common with these characters than those played by Strode, Kitzmiller, or Moreland; he exists as a more fully developed character. In an ensemble film, he emerges as the lead, and not the sort of poorly defined supporting character that is often the norm within most genre films. Perhaps most significant, however, is that Ben's death was the idea of Jones, and not co-writers George Romero and John Russo. In the original script, Ben survives by being rescued by Barbara (Judith O'Dea). Jones felt that Black audiences would rather see his character die, than to have him be rescued by a White woman. In an interview in

Fangoria magazine, Jones is quoted as saying, "I convinced George [Romero] that the Black audience would rather see me dead than saved, after all that had gone on, in a corny and symbolically confusing way."

The 1970s is where things really started getting ugly for the Disposable Brotha. The blaxploitation films that emerged during this time made real the promise of iconic Black heroes like Jim Brown, who went from being a supporting character that died at the service of White heroes, to the main man of the hour that lived to ride off in the sunset. The rise of blaxploitation in the 1970s also created more opportunities for Black performers in films outside the limiting confines of that particular genre, but this participation came with a price. Basically, more films wanted to have some token Black characters to help pull in the newly discovered "special market" of colored audiences, yet these characters were caught in the racial ideology that placed almost no value on Black life. In these non-blaxploitation films, there was still no room for Black heroism to be rewarded with honor and glory alongside White heroes. And it was under these conditions that the Disposable Brotha truly came into his own. The characters killed off in movies like *Dr. No*, *Ice Station Zebra*, *Planet of the Apes* and *Spider Baby* during the 1960s were the prototypes of what would become the archetype of the Disposable Brotha that would populate various genre films throughout the 1970s.

Blaxploitation films had given audiences a newfound hope that super righteous soul brothas could live to see the end of the movie and bask in the victorious glow of kicking ass. That foundation of hope, however, was dealt a devastating blow by one film in particular, *Enter the Dragon*. A martial arts action film starring Bruce Lee, *Enter the Dragon* co-starred karate champion

Jim Kelly as Williams. The personification of 1970s ultra coolness, Williams was a hero right out of the popular blaxploitation films of the time. To be clear, Williams was not a fully developed character. In fact, he was pretty much a mix of well-established blaxploitation stereotypes and clichés. What made the death of Williams so shocking was that by the new set of rules established in blaxploitation he simply wasn't supposed to die. But *Enter the Dragon* showed audiences that no matter how cool, badass, or asskicking a character was—no matter how much his afro was picked to spherical perfection—a brotha was still disposable. Outside the safe confines of the blaxploitation world, the same rules applied in the 1970s: if a Black actor appeared as a token character in a movie, chances were good he or she would be dead before the movie was over. Time and time again we saw it in films like *Damnation Alley, Beware the Blob, The Omega Man, Soylent Green, Psychic Killer, Sisters, Capricorn One, Shivers, Ilsa: Harem Keeper of the Oil Sheiks* and *Alien*, to name a few. One of the most flagrant abusers was the 1973's James Bond film *Live and Let Die*, which managed to kill off almost an entire cast of Black actors.

There were, of course, notable exceptions to the rule of the Disposable Brotha. The *Planet of the Apes* franchise produced two films with Black characters that weren't killed. Within the circles that identified the Disposable Brotha and asked why he was always killed, the character who lived became known as the Brotha That Got Away. Perhaps the two most notable examples of the Brotha That Got Away movies are John Carpenter's *Assault on Precinct 13* and George A. Romero's *Dawn of the Dead*. These films were not only significant for establishing the precedent of not killing the Black guy, but also for casting African American actors as the leading men in roles that defied the stereotypes of the blaxploitation era. These characters were essentially Duane Jones in *Night of the Living Dead*, only they got to live. Austin Stoker, who also survived *Battle for the Planet of the Apes*, starred as a cop in *Assault on Precinct 13*, while Ken Foree went toe-to-toe with an army of zombies in *Dawn of the Dead*, and in the process—by not getting killed—both actors became the symbols of enduring hope. At the same time, it should be mentioned that these characters also existed in predominantly White worlds, which still casts them within the framework of a racial ideology that can only accept Blackness on an individual basis.

By the 1980s, blaxploitation had faded away, leaving Black actors with fewer opportunities for leading roles, relegating many to supporting roles. This reality of the film industry, coupled with a growing conservatism in America that reinvigorated the ideologies of racial inferiority and superiority, created an environment perfect for killing African American characters in the movie. Low budget hack 'em and stack 'em horror movies became the popular choice of the exploitation market, and there was a never-ending stream of Black actors and actresses to play the role of the inevitably ill-fated token Negro. The list of horror, science fiction and action films with Black characters that wind up dead before the final reel is seemingly endless. As both a cinematic cliché and a tired stereotype, the Disposable Brotha thrived and flourished by being made to meet all manner of grisly demise in countless movies. Disposable Brothas even started turning up in films outside the normal confines of where they were usually found. *Rocky IV* got in on the action, killing off Apollo Creed (Carl Weathers) in the classic kill-the-brotha-so-the-White-man-can-avenge-him scenario.

As it had been in the 1970s, there were obvious acceptations to the Disposable Brotha in the 1980s. After giving us the greatest Brotha That Got Away of all time in the form of Ken Foree in *Dawn of the Dead*, George Romero gave us a new hero in the form of Terry Alexander in *Day of the Dead*. But Alexander's status as a BTGA was overshadowed by a new hero that embodied every single cliché of the traditional Disposable Brotha, without dying. On the surface, Winston Zeddemore (Ernie Hudson) was the token Black guy with some great memorable lines in the otherwise all-White cast of *Ghostbusters*, which made him, by every stretch of the imagination, the perfect Disposable Brotha. However, Hudson's character is unique, not just in the fact that he lives, or that his race is, with the exception of one line of dialog, a non-issue. No, the thing that makes Winston Zeddemore such a unique character is that he is the most grounded in reality, and serves as proxy for the audience. As the average guy on the street, looking for

Winston Zeddemore (Ernie Hudson) is *Ghostbusters* is important, not only because he lives, but because he is the character that represents the audience as witness to the supernatural world presented in the film. When Zeddemore joins the team, he is essentially filling in for the audience as the common person. Originally, Eddie Murphy was supposed to play Winston Zeddemore, but the role ended up going to Ernie Hudson.

a job, with no experience with the paranormal, Winston Zeddemore is more like the audience than the other Ghostbusters. In essence, when Zeddemore joins the team, the audience is joining the team. From a standpoint of racial ideology, *Ghostbusters* is a significant film because it not only forces the audience to relate to a Black character, much of the audience's relation to the other characters in the film is filtered through a Black man.

With the home video revolution and the seemingly endless barrage of low budget exploitation schlock flicks, the 1990s and 2000s saw more and more Disposable Brothas in films that got worse and worse. But during this time, a major shift that began with films like *Dawn of the Dead* and *Ghostbusters* took hold, significantly altering the cinematic Graveyard of the Dead Black Characters. This shift culminated with the emergence of Will Smith who, following in the footsteps of actors like Ken Foree and Ernie Hudson, played significant Black characters that did not die. Starting with *Independence Day* and *Men in Black*, Smith began being cast opposite White co-stars, in roles that normally went to White actors, and his characters were not being killed off. Smith's career marks a significant shift in racial ideology, with the mainstream acceptance of a Black man as hero and savior on a large scale. This acceptance, however, doesn't mean that all the lingering notions of race have gone away. In films like *Men in Black*, *Hancock*, and *I, Robot*, Smith's character is one of the few Black people in these cinematic realities, rendering him the exceptional Black individual in otherwise all-White worlds. Likewise, Smith is rarely given a love interest in his films, which has effectively emasculated him. This same emasculation is common amongst many of the Black men who get away at the end of the movie, and represents popular culture's capitulation to the most virulent or racist fears, miscegenation.

Will Smith's emergence as a Brotha That Got Away can be linked to the rise of hip-hop in popular culture, and the move certain rappers made toward the film industry. Building on the sense of empowerment that came as a result of the Civil Rights Movement, and was then filtered through the pop culture lens of blaxploitation, hip-hop helped to change some of the ideological perceptions related to being Black. In the world of hip-hop there was no room for the Disposable Brotha, and this attitude carried over with some of the more popular rappers-turned-actors. LL Cool J lived in *Deep Blue Sea* and *Halloween H20*, Ice Cube survived both *Anaconda* and *Ghosts of Mars*, and miraculously, Busta Rhymes didn't die in *Halloween: Resurrection*. Despite this particular trend, the Disposable Brotha still exists. We are still seeing Black characters getting killed off in films like *The Devil's Rejects*, the *Final Destination* series, remakes of movies like *Friday the 13th* and *Halloween*, and the popular television series *The Walking Dead*. Try counting the number of Disposable Brothas in *The Dark Knight*, and see if you can keep score. Once in a while we see a Brotha That Got Away in movies like *Wrong Turn 2*, but still, after more than five decades and countless movies, we find ourselves asking the same question we've been asking: "Why's the Brotha Gotta Die?" And as with all questions connected to the subject of race, the answer is found within the ideological constructs that determine the worth of human lives based upon the color of skin.

To Be Chinese, Or Not to Be

"The simple truth is that these opinions on such things as racism are traditions, which are nothing more than a "formula" laid down by these elder people's experience. As we progress and time changes, it is necessary to reform this formula." – Bruce Lee

When I was a kid, first traversing the rugged terrain of racial identification, I didn't want to be Black. My understanding of what it meant to be Black—at least my understanding as gleaned from mass media—wasn't something I found particularly interesting. Shows like *Good Times* were downright embarrassing, and though I thrilled to the adventures of the *Six-Million Dollar Man*, or Captain Kirk on *Star Trek* and *Batman*, both in syndicated reruns, I could never be those guys. This fact was pointed out repeatedly by the kids on the playground. "You can't be the Six-Million Dollar Man," they'd say to me. "He's White."

The "he's White" part of these childhood proclamations always felt like a slap in the face. And as an aside, the sting never went away, especially after the phrasing changed. In high school, when telling some friends I was going to learn to play the guitar, one kid scoffed and said, "Niggers can't play guitar." Had his words not transformed me into a five-year-old child, I likely would have taken a swing at him. Instead, I was reduced, as I had been so many other times, to a state of nothingness, in which I could not be the hero, or the guitar player in a rock band, or much of anything else because, well, I wasn't White.

Growing up, measuring my life and my aspirations by the stick of popular culture, it felt like my options were limited. On television and in comic books I searched for Black characters that I could either identify with, or aspire to be. I had yet to discover the larger-than-life heroes of blaxploitation films, and as a result, I came up short. I suppose it is because of this, in some way, shape, or form, that I wanted to be Chinese. Or perhaps I should be more clear, because I didn't want to be Chinese as much as I wanted to be Bruce Lee.

When, where, and how I first became aware of Bruce Lee is something of a mystery. As near as I can tell, he's just one of those people that I always knew who he was—like my grandparents, Muhammad Ali, and God. Inevitably, this speaks to the power of mass media and popular culture, even in the days when there was only a few channels on television, the Internet was something unheard of, and research meant cracking open an encyclopedia. Looking back, it almost seems that if you were a kid growing up in the 1970s, you knew who Bruce Lee was simply through the power of mass consciousness—that collective group awareness that drives the thought process of much of society. Whatever the reason may be, Lee was something of a constant in my life—as well as many other young people—and to a large extent one of the key contributors to a new phase in the evolution of racial identification for many African Americans.

In America, Bruce Lee was the most recognizable actor in the kung fu movies produced out of Hong Kong that started playing in the United States in the early 1970s. Lee had already built a following of fans in America with his co-starring role on the television series *Green Hornet,* as well as a few other notable appearances in film and television. But stardom in America was elusive for Lee, who as an Asian had the misfortune of not being White, which made him unmarketable as a leading man in eyes of Hollywood. Lee eventually returned to Hong Kong, where producer Raymond Chow cast him in a series of low budget films. Chow's Golden Harvest Studios was the chief competitor of Shaw Brothers Studios, Hong Kong's biggest film production company, and the main producer of kung fu movies in the 1970s. Without realizing it, Bruce Lee, Golden Harvest, and Shaw Brothers were providing African American audiences the resources to better understand themselves, and along with the blaxploitation films of the era, changed how many of us see ourselves.

There's been a fair amount written about blaxploitation (much of it by me), though when all is said and done, it remains a largely misunderstood and maligned part of film history. Blaxploitation, along with kung fu movies, laid a foundation for what would become a significant challenge to the established racial ideologies entrenched in popular culture (and ultimately contributing to

Enduring the humiliation of cultural imperialism, Bruce Lee fought back against his oppressors in *The Chinese Connection* (a.k.a. *Fist of Fury*), and in doing so became the hero of the oppressed. Lee help popularize Hong Kong-produced kung fu films in America, which were especially popular with Black audiences who related to the messages of anti-colonialism and the overall asskicking.

the birth of hip-hop). And this is not to say that this new foundation was not without problems, but that does not change the fact that blaxploitation, and much less obviously kung fu movies, redefined the filters through which Blacks were presented and perceived in popular culture. This transformation, which played out in movie theaters, drive-ins, on television, and the burgeoning home video market of the 1980s, would have a tremendous impact on Black youth. The result was that many of us either wanted to be Chinese, a private detective, a pimp, or some combination thereof.

Whether it is on a conscious or a subconscious level, the power of popular culture should never be underestimated. The things that are frequently dismissed as frivolous, disposable works of entertainment also serve as tools of propaganda in helping set and reinforce different ideologies. This is especially true of television and film, which are often mistaken as being reflections of reality, as opposed to artificial constructs. Even people who can recognize television shows and movies as manufactured works, and not as being real, often fail to see the ideological constructs upon which these texts have been built. Understanding this is crucial in understanding how various works of mass media and art can reflect and contest accepted ideologies and socio-political forms.

Take for example the racist film *The Birth of a Nation*. It not only reflected the accepted ideologies of the time, it spawned a counter-movement of films that challenged the ideologies in question. In response to D.W. Griffith's pro-Ku Klux Klan, an entire industry of separate cinema for Black audiences emerged. These films reflected sentiments in direct opposition to the ideologies of White supremacy found in *The Birth of a Nation*, helping to usher in a growing movement of pride in the Black community that was played out in motion pictures. Films by Black directors like Oscar Michaeaux, Noble Johnson, and Spencer Williams, became an escape from the escape of mainstream films that marginalized and dehumanized Blacks, serving as an affirmation of equality. This growing cinematic niche coincided with the Harlem Renaissance, and the growing political movement of the time, creating within the Black community a sense of identity outside of what was dictated by the pervasive ideology of White America. This sense of identity would go through numerous transformations both politically and artistically, politically culminating in the Civil Rights Movement of the 1950s and 1960s, and cinematically culminating in the early 1970s with the cycle of films known as blaxploitation.

By the mid twentieth century, film had become the most popular form of entertainment, creating a new type of mythology within the construct of cinema. Mythology and myth creation is a crucial part of the development of all cultures, and as Joseph Campbell (1988) explains, "Myth helps you to put your mind in touch with this experience of being alive. It tells you what the experience is" (p. 6). The mythology that emerged out of American cinema purported to reflect the ideals of American life and heroism. This cinematic mythology, however, largely excluded everyone except White men, and as a result, failed to convey the experience of being alive to a rather large cross-section of the population. The emergence of blaxploitation, in the wake of the political and socio-economic changes of the Civil Rights Movement, is best defined as fantasy fulfillment and the creation of myths specific to the Black audience. These films provided a pop culture representation that was not reflective of reality so much as reflective of a cultural need for heroes and mythology. The popularity of blaxploitation was in large part because these films provided cinematic confrontation to, and defeat of, the systemic racist ideologies that defined much of the Black experience in America.

The frequent message of fighting back against the system of oppression resonated with Black American audiences, but that message was not limited to blaxploitation films, and could be found in the popular culture of other countries. This is where Bruce Lee and kung fu movies come into the picture of Black liberation and self-identification, with a series of poorly dubbed and easily dismissed action films, which addressed such universal concepts as the desire of the oppressed to usurp the oppressor. Even though these films were produced in another country, in another language, for a foreign culture, and were released in America simply as a means of exploiting the B-movie market, an intrinsic connection developed between the Hong Kong kung fu movies and American audiences, particularly Black American audiences. This is how I, and many like me, came to want to be Chinese.

As a predominantly Chinese-populated colony of both Japan and Britain, Hong Kong long suffered the effects of colonization and colonialism, as well as cultural imperialism. The book *MediaMaking: Mass Media in a Popular Culture* defines cultural imperialism as "the idea that if one could control the culture of another people—then one could easily control the people themselves" (p. 427). Through cultural imperialism, Chinese culture in Hong Kong took a back seat to the culture of its occupiers. During the occupation of Hong Kong by the Japanese, and for twenty years after the fact, Japanese cultural imperialism factored heavily in popular entertainment, resulting in

104

films that catered more to Japanese sensibilities than to Chinese. But by the mid 1960s, production companies in Hong Kong such as Shaw Brothers began making films more reflective of Chinese culture, including *Come Drink With Me*, *The One-Armed Swordsman*, and *The Chinese Boxer*. Within many of these films, defiance against Japanese imperialism is a recurring narrative convention.

Kung fu movies first started showing up in the United States in the early 1970s—just as the blaxploitation film was emerging. These exhibitions of Chinese martial arts primarily played in theaters located in the Chinatown district of larger cities like New York and San Francisco, and in decaying inner-city theaters where they often played as part of a double feature with blaxploitation films. To the outside observer, these disparate genres of film had nothing in common other than action and violence, while in reality there was quite a bit in common. Both genres were largely comprised of revenge fantasies aimed at an audience of the oppressed. Despite obvious differences, the intended target audiences for both blaxploitation movies in America and kung fu films in Hong Kong were, in fact, quite similar. Sundiata Keita Cha-Jua (2008) explains that "ideological discourses, sociohistorical context, and the similarities in the narrative structures of blaxploitation and kung fu films predisposed African Americans toward Hong Kong martial arts films" (p. 215). In fact, it is the underlying themes of liberation that not only made kung fu films so popular; it is why many of these films have endured over the years. M.T Kato (2007) writes, "What made the kung fu film boom during the late 1960s and 1970s a popular cultural revolution instead of a mere commercial celebration of Chinese nationalism was the allegory of the imperial and colonial power and decolonization struggles" (p. 11).

One of the most significant of the early kung fu films to play in America was the Shaw Brothers production *Five Fingers of Death*. A commercial success in the United States, *Five Fingers of Death* was crucial in generating interest in martial arts and paved the way for Bruce Lee, who emerged as a global superstar with the film *The Big Boss* and *Fist of Fury*, which was released in the United States under the title *The Chinese Connection*. *The Chinese Connection* was not only phenomenally successful; it was deeply entrenched in the anti-Japanese imperialism messages of the era. Cut from similar cloth as the empowerment fantasies of blaxploitation films, *Five Fingers of Death*, *The Chinese Connection*, and the other kung fu movies to follow, all resonated with Black audiences, either consciously or

Lieh Lo stars in *Five Fingers of Death* (a.k.a. *King Boxer*), one of the first kung fu movies released in the United States by Hong Kong's Shaw Brothers Productions. *Five Fingers of Death* was a tremendous hit in America, and is one of the key films responsible for popularizing martial arts movies in the U.S.

106

subconsciously, providing a new form of mythology. Adding to the popularity of the Hong Kong action film was the fact that the heroes—like those populating blaxploitation films—were not Caucasian. Although Bruce Lee's martial arts films were not the first to play in America, he was the first global martial arts superstar, and incredibly popular in the Black community.

Set in Shanghai during the Japanese occupation, *The Chinese Connection* stars Bruce Lee as the fictional Chen Zhen, student of the real life martial arts master and folk hero Huo Yuanjia. When Chen Zhen attempts to enter a park, he is stopped, and pointed toward a sign that reads, "No Dogs and Chinese Allowed." This sign, of course, recalls the "Whites Only" and "No Blacks Allowed" signs found through various parts of the United States just a few years earlier. The sting of humiliation born out of exclusion, the soul-crushing dehumanization felt by the oppressed, proved to be so universal that it transcended nationality and culture. Black audiences in America understood the "No Dogs and Chinese Allowed" sign in a way that eluded most White audiences—its message resonating on a level that seemed to tell us we were not alone in a world that did not want us. And so, when Chen Zhen beats the crap out of some Japanese men who offer to take him into the park—provided he act like a dog—and then smashes the sign, he became a mythological hero of the oppressed. The fact that Chen Zhen wasn't White—that he was some type of other—made him have even more in common with Black audiences. This is why so many Black kids wanted to be Chinese.

I was first introduced to martial arts and kung fu movies during the initial wave of releases in 1970s, which first sparked my curiosity. Though my mother was liberal in her parental guidance practices when it came to movies, this policy did not extent to kung fu movies, and as a result I saw very few in the theaters during the 1970s. I did become more familiar with these movies in the 1980s, however, when a series of films were collected into a package and syndicated for television. This syndication deal, which broadcast dozens of anti-colonialist kung fu movies to television stations throughout the United States, marked the second significant exposure of Hong Kong action films to an American audience.

Just as the first wave of kung fu movies in the 1970s had captured the imagination of audiences at inner city theaters and rural drive-ins across America, so too did the second wave, collected in packages with names like *Black Belt Theater* and *Kung Fu Theater*. And in some ways, this particular exposure was more significant. For one thing, the films were delivered into American homes for free, at a time when there were fewer channel options and the home video revolution was still in its infancy. When Shaw Brothers film *36th Chamber of Shaolin* was edited for television and broadcast as

Gordon Liu stars as San Te in the Shaw Brothers production *36th Chamber of Shaolin* (a.k.a. *Master Killer*), one of many Hong Kong-produced kung fu movies that played in America during the 1970s and 1980s. Black audiences related to the heroes in these films because they fought back against their oppressors, and in doing so developed knowledge of self. Heroes like San Te always learned of their history outside the context of oppression.

Master Killer on a Saturday afternoon in 1981, there was not much else on television. I still remember watching *Master Killer* for the first time and being mesmerized. Perhaps it was because I was older, and capable of deeper critical analysis, but for whatever reason, *Master Killer* resonated with me on a far deeper level than the handful of kung fu movies I had convinced my mom to take me to see when I was younger. This particular movie opened me up to a new type of film, a new culture, and though I did not fully comprehend it at the time, an expanded understanding of cultural oppression.

Some people fail to comprehend how and why kung fu films became so important, especially to African American audiences, and it is this failure that speaks to an even greater lack of understanding surrounding the Black community. The fact of the matter is that in order to understand or explain why kung fu movies were important to Black people—as with all things dealing with race in America—there must be a close examination of historical contexts. There are several fundamental reasons for the popularity and impact of kung fu films with Black audiences in America. The first reasons were present during the initial rise of popularity in the 1970s, when these films brought messages of liberation and revenge fantasies to audiences, often paired with similar themed blaxploitation movies. But despite some similarities, there were some significant differences between blaxploitation and kung fu. One of these key differences is clarified, rather succinctly, by hip-hop star RZA (2009), who writes in his memoir "the only knowledge the media showed about black history was about either slaves or pimps—*Roots, The Mack,* and that was basically it. So in a way, films like *The Thirty-sixth Chamber* reflected our experience and solidified it, drew people like me into the truth of our own history" (p. 53).

It may be difficult to understand how RZA, a Black man born in Brooklyn, New York, can watch a film like *36th Chamber of Shaolin* (a.k.a. *Master Killer*) and see a reflection of the African American experience in a movie set in 18th century China, or find some sort of truth that relates to Black history. RZA's observation and reactions to *36th Chamber of Shaolin*—and to many kung fu movies, as his memoir discusses—is a result of globalization. As explained by cultural theorist Stuart Hall, "globalization involves the transformation of every local culture into a hybrid that already includes elements from many different cultures...the commonality of globalization is that every culture is a hybrid—though each culture is a hybrid in a different way, as the result of different power struggles and historical circumstances" (p. 444).

This theory of globalization helps to explain the popularity of kung fu

Grandmaster Flash and the Furious Five, part of the growing movement of artistic expression that emerged out of New York City in the 1970s and 1980s, which would go on to become known as hip-hop. Heavily influenced by blaxploitation and kung fu movies, hip-hop marked a significant change in racial identification, while continuing to make a commodity of being Black.

films in the Black American community, and the lasting cultural impact. As RZA pointed out in his memoir, the mass media representation of Blacks in America has long been limited to a very narrow spectrum of images—due in large part to persistent racial ideologies formed by decades of propaganda. Even within the liberation afforded by the fantasy projections of blaxploitation films, the representation of Blacks was still limited to a very small number of options. Within the context of blaxploitation, the larger body of film, and other mass media—as well as historical texts—the predominant prescribed role for Blacks in America is as one of the oppressed, with almost no other contextual frame of reference. That is to say that the heroes of blaxploitation films existed in a world with no history. Cinematic heroes like Shaft and Foxy Brown had no historical cultural ties, be they to slavery or Africa, and merely existed as the oppressed fighting back against the oppressor. The role of the oppressed in kung fu movies existed within a larger, richer contextual framework, creating a more culturally rich experience than blaxploitation movies. For Black audiences, it was easy enough to relate to the oppressed characters in kung fu movies, because like them, the characters were not White. The characters in kung fu movies, however, drew from a deeper source of cultural influences and nationalism that was frequently all too absent from blaxploitation films.

As a film critic and a pop culture historian, I've watched hundreds of blaxploitation movies and kung fu films, but for years I wondered why I always related more to the heroes of the kung fu pictures. What I came to realize through years of close observation and critical analysis was exactly what RZA wrote of in his personal memoir: within kung fu films there was a deeper expression of truth and knowledge of self that reflected both my personal and cultural history. Take for example *36th Chamber of Shaolin*, considered by many critics to be one of the greatest martial arts movies ever made. The film stars Gordon Liu as San Te, a student who becomes the victim of the oppressive Manchus. San Te seeks refuge in the Shaolin temple, hoping to learn kung fu to seek revenge against the Manchus who killed his friend. But as he masters the thirty-five learning chambers of the Shaolin temple, the older monks at the temple also teach San Te about his cultural history, and he begins to develop a greater knowledge of self, understanding his role as one of the oppressed masses, and the history outside the context of oppression. This insight allows San Te to see that true power comes not from knowing how to fight for revenge, but how to fight for justice and the liberation of the oppressed. When he completes his training in the thirty-fifth chamber, he leaves the temple to start a thirty-sixth chamber, one that brings the greatest weapon of all to the oppressed people—the self awareness to understand themselves outside the paradigm of oppression.

The characters in kung fu movies like *36th Chamber of Shaolin* existed in a cinematic fantasy world where revenge is interwoven with attaining a higher level of self awareness, there were always lessons to be learned, and historical context to draw from in which the oppressed were not always oppressed. This is knowledge of self. By comparison, blaxploitation movies were generally revenge fantasies that started and stopped with the acts of vengeance. Films like *Sweet Sweetback's Baaadasssss Song* were about the revenge of the oppressed, but there was no deep historical analysis of the characters outside of the paradigm of oppression. In other words, blaxploitation heroes delivered the revenge, but the greater, transcendent knowledge of self their kung fu brethren attained was nowhere to be found. This is essentially why I found myself drawn to the heroes of kung fu movies more than blaxploitation heroes. Kung fu heroes were all oppressed, but they came from worlds in which there was history predating oppression, and they always learned something profound about themselves before they killed the bad guys. In order for blaxploitation heroes to reach a similar level as the heroes of kung fu movies, inevitably they would have had to deal with the deeper context of their oppression, and go back to a time before being oppressed. In other words, blaxploitation heroes had little to no knowledge of self.

It is difficult for many Americans to acquire knowledge of self, due in large part to the fragmented and incomplete way in which history is taught and understood. This is true for the descendants of African slaves, whose history exists all-too-often as an abstract concept that is incomplete. It is also true, however, for most White Americans—whether descended from slave owners or not—because they are also tied to slavery, either directly, or simply through ideological constructs. For many Americans, any semblance of knowledge of self is predicated on an understanding of slavery, and the reconciliation of the role it played in shaping how they are indentified. Because slavery and the racial ideologies surrounding it have never been adequately addressed on a national level, a large number of Americans lack knowledge of self. These people do not fully understand themselves, and in the quest to better understand life, they turn, as humans have done throughout time, to mythology as a means of explaining their existence. Unfortunately, in America, our myths have been recorded in the language of cinema, and largely informed by a fractured and distorted historical narrative that is corrupted by ideological constructs of superiority and inferiority.

Blaxploitation provided Black audiences with revenge fantasies against the ideological constructs of oppression, without ever providing a true historical context of why revenge was needed. Kung fu films provided audiences with an understanding that the oppressed had a history that extended beyond oppression, and that justice, not revenge, is the only way to end that oppression. Both genres of films, easily dismissed by critics, academics, and highbrow intellectuals delivered to a select audience the subversive message of challenging your oppressor. If for no other reason, those films were valuable beyond measure, in that they taught a select group of people that it was possible to fight back, and in the process attain a greater understanding of yourself. I know this, because I was part of that audience, and I saw what emerged from the shadow of these anti-colonialist kung fu movies and anti-hero blaxploitation flicks. Kung fu and blaxploitation films were key antecedents in the evolution of what is arguably one of the most significant pop culture phenomena of the last forty years. I am, of course, referring to the cultural movement known as hip-hop.

The culture of hip-hop has its roots in mid-to-late 1970s New York City, just after the initial blaxploitation and kung fu craze, and before the syndication of kung fu movies on television. Before the culture even had a name, groups of young people—primarily poor Blacks and Hispanics—were experimenting with music, art, dance, and fashion in ways that both expressed life in the low-income inner-city, as well as offering some sort of symbolic escape from the restrictive confines of life in the ghetto. These experimentations led to graffiti as a form of public art—an attack on bourgeoisie values and the accepted definition of what art could and could not be. The same applied to music and dance. Music was created by DJs taking bits and pieces of other songs, and mixing them together to create new songs that MCs would sing or rap over. Meanwhile, dancers would combine moves from a wide variety of sources, including popular steps seen on the television series *Soul Train*, classic routines from performers like the Nicholas Brothers, and the fight choreography from kung fu movies. All of this began to coalesce into a social movement that by the early 1980s had formed into an actual subculture of poor, inner city America.

From the very beginning, hip-hop was an extension of the anti-establishment, anti-oppression themes found in both blaxploitation and kung fu movies. If those movies spoke *to* a specific generation and culture as a reflection of their rage, then hip-hop actually spoke *for* a generation and culture as a manifestation of their rage. It was an idea of anti-colonialism made real and given a voice, with its own music and dance. The popularity of hip-hop is that it is a means of expression that gave voice to the voiceless. When I was asked by Andrew Rausch (2011) to write the foreword to his book *I Am Hip-Hop* and define what hip-hop was, I wrote, "Hip-hop, in all of its permutations, is the creation of something from nothing. It is the transformation of ugliness into beauty. It is a defiant stance against a society that seeks to marginalize the poor and disenfranchised, only to find that the poor and disenfranchised have created their own kingdom" (p. viii).

As a form of expression for a particular subculture, hip-hop is forever connected to entertainment, placing it at the crossroads of culture and capitalism. As I grow older, I recognize the dangers to be found in this precarious intersection, and more easily see the same patterns of racial identification that have always plagued Black America. Hip-hop, or perhaps more importantly, rap music, which is processed and sold as hip-hop, has become a key identifier of what it means to be Black, but this identity is in and of itself a byproduct of capitalism. Once again, the identity of Black people is being defined within the context of a commodity that is bought, sold, and traded. In other words, hip-hop, in the form of rap music, has become in many ways what slavery used to be, a means of determining the worth of a people through what it is they can produce within the framework of ideological demands. Ultimately, this means that while hip-hop once spoke for us, telling others how we defined ourselves, as a byproduct of capitalism it now speaks to us, telling us what we are supposed to be.

Identification, whether it is racial, gender, cultural, or any other type imaginable, is supposed to give each of us a better understanding of what we are. Through genetics and environment we inherit key identifiers, and then spend our lives trying to live as what it is we've been identified as being. When in doubt, we will look around us, at our family, our neighborhood, our community, looking for examples of how to be what we're told we are. If more doubt remains, we will look to the popular culture representations that serve as an escape from the uncertainty of our existence, while somehow offering a deceptive reassurance of what reality should look like. And for some people, this process works, as they find a way to identify themselves by the world around them, and the pop culture interpretations of that world.

116

But what about the people that this process doesn't work for? What about the people who watch reality television and recognize that what is being shown is not real? What about the people who realize that the love in love songs is not the same as love in real life? What about the people who immerse themselves in hip-hop to better understand what it means to be black, only to discover that being black and hip-hop are not the same things?

If there is one thing I have learned over the years, it is this: figuring out who you are can be difficult. Every culture, society, religion, race, gender, and whatever you want to list as a means of identification, has some set of criteria used to define "normal." Unfortunately, I've never met anyone who meets these standards. None of us is normal, and no matter how hard we may try, we will never fully fit in. Yet we still go on, trying to figure out who we are by using definitions created by other people. For me, it has been a lifetime of desperately seeking to define myself racially amidst my own racial ambiguity. I have given my life to scholarship, critical analysis, and the dogged pursuit of finding a place to call home racially, and even then, I don't feel like I belong.

Ultimately, the quest we should all be on is one that allows us to reclaim our humanity, and in the process evolve as human beings. In order to do this, we must be willing to look beyond all existing identifiers, and resign ourselves to the fact that who we are must start from within. This means that we must decide for ourselves who we are, which can be a daunting prospect.

Worlds Without Color

"There's this idea that monsters don't have reflections in a mirror. And what I've always thought isn't that monsters don't have reflections in a mirror. It's that if you want to make a human being into a monster, deny them, at the cultural level, any reflection of themselves." – Junot Diaz

The first time I saw The *Wizard of Oz* was back in the 1970s during one of its theatrical re-releases. Before the home video revolution of 1980s, the only way to see older movies was if they were broadcast on television, or if they enjoyed a theatrical re-release. Frequently, classic movies would be pulled out of the vaults, and dropped into movie theaters across the country, which is how I came to see *The Wizard of Oz* for the first time. It was, for me, one of those incredible moments of childhood, filled with a sense of wonder. Even though the film was more than thirty years old at the time, its lavish production mesmerized me, and I became hooked. Fortunately, *The Wizard of Oz* was also a staple of television, where it was broadcast once a year, right around Christmas, making it an annual tradition for me.

I'm not sure when it happened, but some time during my second or third viewing of *The Wizard of Oz*, I noticed something a bit disturbing to me. Unless you counted the Wicked Witch, who was green, there were no people of color in Oz. And by people of color, what I mean to say is that there were no people that looked like me or my family in the magical land of Oz. All of those Munchkins, and none of them were Black, or Asian, or

Hispanic, or Native American. I'm six or seven years-old, sitting in front of the television, and it hits me like a ton of bricks that Munchkinland has nothing but White people. Surely, this must have been a mistake. Even at my all-White elementary school, there were five or six Black kids, myself included. By the time Dorothy and her companions got to the Emerald City, I was certain they'd see at least one Black person. The scene where the Tin Man is getting scrubbed and polished would have to have Black people, because it essentially took place at a car wash, and the car wash was pretty much the one place I knew that only employed Black people. But there was no Black people washing the Tin Man, and the Cowardly

One of the most popular films of all time, *The Wizard of Oz*, does not have a single person of color in the cast (unless you count the Wicked Witch, who is green). This is oppression through omission, in which people of color are simply rendered nonexistent in the reality presented within the film. You would be surprised how often this happens in film and television.

Lion was at a beauty parlor, and there were no Black women with hot combs straightening his hair. The truth about Oz became painfully clear: it was an all-White world—except for green witches, of course.

Shortly after I made my starting discovery about Oz, the Broadway musical *The Wiz* made its debut. *The Wiz* was a retelling of *The Wizard of Oz* (which itself was an adaptation of L. Frank Baum's *The Wonderful Wizard of Oz*), that featured an all-Black cast, and a contemporary musical score steeped in the traditions of gospel, soul, and funk. Growing up a train ride from New York City meant that commercials for *The Wiz* aired on television all the time, with the announcer proclaiming, "*The Wiz* is a wow!" I, however, did not believe that *The Wiz* could be a wow, and more importantly, I didn't believe that Oz, in any incarnation, should have Black people.

I know that may sound strange, given that just a short time before *The Wiz* made its debut I had noticed the lack of diversity in *The Wizard of Oz*, but the truth is that in a very short time, I had simply come to accept what was being told to me: there are some places where Black people just don't belong. This is, in fact, the message that countless movies and television shows have broadcast to the masses, by simply excluding people of color from the reality created within their context. It doesn't seem like much, but as time goes by, and you watch more movies and more TV shows, and you see either no people of color, or only one or two in the background, it unconsciously conditions you to accept that the worlds seen in works of popular entertainment are all-White. And this is why *The Wiz* sounded like the stupidest thing in the world to me. There was no way Dorothy could be Black, because Black people don't look like Dorothy—or the Scarecrow,

The original Broadway production of *The Wiz* created a world for Black characters where they had normally been excluded.

or the Tin Man, or the Lion, or anyone else in Oz.

When we talk about Blacks in film (and television), the conversation tends to revolve around the negative roles, steeped in clichés and stereotypes that feed into the already existing ideologies of race. For much of its relatively short history, the motion picture industry has stuck to a very narrow spectrum of Black characterizations, which it has used over and over again, creating a recognizable and enduring cinematic legacy. James Snead (2004) explains, "Because film is infinitely repeatable, and it records and preserves images, that film will never change, and because viewers see that film as denoting an unchanging truth about blacks, they will always be able to believe in that image" (p. 140). Where Snead is going with his observation is the same place many other critics, historians, and theorists have gone—that the repeated use of the same characterizations and stereotypes leads to an acceptance of these representations as being the truth about Black people. If this is true—and to a large extent I do believe it is—then what sort of truth about Blacks is created from our repeated absence in movies and other works of pop culture?

An incredible amount of attention has been paid to the way Blacks are portrayed in film (and television), and the way these portrayals affect the perception of African Americans. Likewise, there has been much said about the lack of participation of Blacks in the film and television industry—both in front of and behind the camera—that in and of itself speaks to a wide range of issues surrounding racial ideology. There is no denying that racial ideology has played a significant part in the way Blacks are portrayed in movies, as well as the involvement of African Americans on all levels in the world of film. But the thing that is seldom talked about—at least not to the extent that it has ever really come to my attention—is the phenomena of omission as a form of oppression. Yes, plenty has been said about there not being enough people of color in films, but not nearly as much has been written about the impact of there being no people of color in specific movies, and the perception of reality that it creates. This leads me back to *The Wizard of Oz*.

Originally released in 1939, *The Wizard of Oz* is one of the most beloved movies of all time. Multiple theatrical releases, decades of regular broadcast on television, and home video have made it one of the most widely seen movies in the history of cinema, especially amongst children and families. And in this magical world, there is not a single person of color. Sure, the easy explanation is that *The Wizard of Oz* came out in 1939, and that was pretty much how things were. But what does that really mean? Well, it means that in the 1930s it was perfectly acceptable to not have people of color on screen, because at that time ideologies of racial inferiority and superiority still prevailed. It means that rather than offend the racist sensibilities of some audience members by including people of color in the cast of the movie, the producers of *The Wizard of Oz* created a reality that was all White. This sends a message to every child of color who watches the movie that they have no place in this particular world, and it sends a message to every White child that a world without diversity is perfectly fine. This is omission and oppression by way of accepted cultural norms. And that is racism, whether or not *The Wizard of Oz* itself is racist.

It would be one thing if *The Wizard of Oz* were merely one movie guilty of oppression through omission, or if it were only films from older eras more steeped in the racial ideologies of the past; but that's just not the case. Take for example director Peter Jackson's immensely popular *Lord of the Rings* trilogy, released more than six decades after *The Wizard of Oz*. Here we have a film series, with a collective running time of more than nine hours, set in a fantasy world populated by humans, elves, hobbits, and all other sorts of make-believe characters, and every single one of these characters is White. From what I can see, in all of Middle Earth, there is not one recognizable person of color to be found anywhere. The closest thing to people of color to be found in the *Lord of the Rings* movies are the orcs, which only plays into the most ugly of stereotypes of Blacks dating back to films like *The Birth of a Nation*.

There are those that will no doubt defend the *Lord of the Rings* movies with any number of justifications, the most innocent and innocuous being, "Hey, its just an imaginary world, so what's the big deal if there aren't any people of color?" The big deal is that even though *Lord of the Rings* is set in a make-believe world, it is accepted by audiences as being a real world within its cinematic context. In fact, the success or failure of any film hinges on the audience's ability and willingness to accept what they are seeing on the screen is real or true within the context it exists. This does not mean that audiences believe that Middle Earth or Oz are real places that can be visited, it just means that audiences suspend their disbelief enough to engage with the film as if these places are real. By accepting Oz or Middle Earth as being real within their cinematic framework, the audience also accepts all that is contained within these worlds. And if there are no people of color in these worlds, it means that the audience is accepting of a world that has no place for people of color, which in turn creates a desensitization to a lack of diversity, or in some cases a rejection of diversity. This is what happened to me when I first heard about *The Wiz*.

When *The Wiz* first debuted on Broadway I was about eight-years-old, and by that point I had become so used to worlds without Black people, that I had started to think it was normal. *The Wiz* made no sense to me, and sounded like a bad idea, because I had been conditioned to think of that particular type of reality as not including Black people. This is what happens with omission of entire groups of people for prolonged periods of time. And as bad as it is for Blacks, it is far worse for Native Americans and other groups, whose level of omission runs much deeper. By not seeing images that reflect ourselves in these realities projected upon the screen, our very existence is compromised. It is as if we don't exist, because there is no one in Oz that looks like us—and in turn we become dehumanized. This dehumanization is just another extension of the same dehumanization that justified slavery and the genocide of Native Americas. We were robbed of our right to be human in this country, and then as a type of mythology emerged in the form of motion pictures, we were either misrepresented—further dehumanizing us—or we were denied visibility, making us non-existent in the realm of story and myth.

The purpose of mythology and story is to explain the existence and experiences of humans. Story and myth are the ways in which we process and express who we are and what we've experienced. It doesn't matter if these experiences are triumphs or tragedies; there is an innate human need to tell stories to make sense of our lives. It is through story and myth that we define who we are in relation to all that surrounds us, or has happened to us, and helps us deal with the traumas we have endured. The problem in the United States, however, is that the stories and myths used to explain the American existence are informed by the racial ideologies that dehumanize people of color. This results in a mythological construct that either dehumanizes people of color, as is the case with The *Birth of Nation*, or ignores them all together, as is the case with *The Wizard of Oz* and *Lord of the Rings*, which in turn dehumanizes through omission.

America is a nation built on racism, genocide and, by default, the trauma experienced by those who endured the racism and genocide. The stories that emerged as a means to convey the building of this nation sought reconciliation for the terrible acts of dehumanization perpetrated on African slaves and Native Americans by either perpetuating the dehumanization, or leaving the victims out of the narrative. This practice of dehumanization or omission of people of color took hold within the mass media and pop culture texts of post-Civil War America, and carried over into the world of cinema. Jannette Dates and William Barlow (1990) explain, "In American society, by reproducing the ideological hegemony of the dominant white culture, the mass media help to legitimate the inequalities in class and race relations" (p. 4). In other words, the dominant majority in America—White people—came to grips with the multigenerational trauma they inflicted on people of color by simply creating a lie and choosing to believe the lie. This behavior is called cognitive dissonance, a term used to describe the psychological conflict that emerges when there is conflict between behavior and thought. Dr. Joy DeGruy (2005) writes:

> During the past 500 years Europeans have spent significant resources to 'prove' Africans and those of African descent are inferior. The difference between the actions of the Euro-peans (i.e., enslaving, raping, and killing) and their beliefs about themselves (i.e., 'We are good Christians') was so

126

great and the cognitive dissonance so painful, that they were obliged to go to great lengths in order to survive their own horrific behavior. (p. 52)

To a large extent, the film industry is merely an extension of the cognitive dissonance that has developed in place of reconciliation over past deeds. This is why there are no people of color in The *Wizard of Oz* or *Lord of the Rings*, not because either is especially racist, but because the cognitive dissonance used to reconcile racism is so strong that it spills over into popular culture. I realize that this may sound ridiculous, but stop for a moment, and consider how many popular movies have no people of color in the cast, for no reason other than they simply don't exist in that particular world. The first *Star Wars* has no people of color. *The Princess Bride* has no people of color. *E.T. the Extra-terrestrial* has no people of color. *When Harry Met Sally* has no people of color. Disney's *Snow White and the Seven Dwarves*, *Alice in Wonderland*, and *Cinderella* have no cartoon people of color. The list goes on and on, filled with blockbusters and award-winners, and the one thing they all have in common is that they all exist in worlds populated solely by White people, which means they all perpetuate oppression through omission.

As difficult as it is to discuss race and racism, it is even more difficult to discuss racism where there are no outright signs of it existing, as is the case with oppression through omission. Indeed, it is incredibly difficult to look at a film like *The Princess Bride* or *The Breakfast Club* and accuse either of being racist, because neither demonstrates outward or overt racism. At the same time, neither film has a single character of color, nor is there any reason for this exclusion. The problem, of course, is that there are hundreds, if not thousands

The first *Star Wars* and *The Princess Bride* are perfect examples of oppression through omission. Neither film is necessarily racist, and yet neither film has a single person of color in the cast (not even extras in the background). There is no real reason for this level of wholesale exclusion, yet there it is, and it is found in countless films and television shows. Over time, this type of exclusion becomes a form of oppression, which is the manifestation of a racist ideology. It doesn't matter that these films are not racist, because they are informed by an ideological construct that results in the creation of cinematic realities in which people of color have no place, rendering them nonexistent. Now, imagine being a child of color growing up in America, and seldom seeing characters like yourself in popular entertainment. What would that do to your perception of your place in the world?

of movies, with nary a character of color, and no real reason for their exclusion. And the accumulated effect of all of these movies is the constant creation of realities that are accepted as being exclusive to White people, without any question. When worlds without diversity are normal—even within the artificial framework of a movie—it then becomes that much more difficult to accept diversity as being normal or healthy in the real world. This then becomes a form of cultural hegemony—the domination of other cultures by a single ruling culture or class.

A few years after *The Wiz* debuted on Broadway, I was fortunate enough to see it. By this time I was about ten-years-old, and I was still convinced that it would be a stupid play. I simply could not imagine Black people in any way, shape, or form in the *Wizard of Oz*. But something truly amazing happened while watching *The Wiz*, I realized that Dorothy could be Black, as could the Scarecrow, the Tin Man, and the Lion. What had seemed stupid and impossible to me had suddenly become very real. At the time, I could not have explained it, other than to say that I thought the play was one of the coolest things I had ever seen in my life. But what I came to realize many years later was that *The Wiz* had been a crucial step in the restoration of the humanity that had been largely denied to myself and other African Americans. It was one of the first times I saw a world completely populated by Black folks, that wasn't *Good Times* or *What's Happening*, in which the characters existed outside of the narrow ideological confines I had already started to identify.

There is a feeling of recognition and identification that occurs when audiences connect with characters they see in films and television. Blacks, women, and other people of color are denied aspects of this sense of recognition, when the characters they are asked to identify with look nothing like them. That is not to say that differences in race, gender, or ethnicity make it impossible to identify with other characters, because that's not the case. In fact, in America we have been conditioned to identify with White people—especially White men—as being the hero. This conditioning, however, is merely part of the ongoing racial ideology that places White men in a role of superiority, and everyone else, with a few notable exceptions, in roles of inferiority. And as long as these ideological constructs remain intact, audiences of color and women will continue to be oppressed.

The worlds without color that spring up throughout the universe that we call popular entertainment are not necessarily racist in and of themselves. At the same time, they are reflections of lingering ideologies that dehumanize people of color. This must be recognized, discussed, and addressed as a serious problem. It is the responsibility of the creators of these worlds to populate them with individuals that cultivate diversity. But in bringing diversity to these worlds, creators also need to make sure that these diverse characters are fully developed in their humanity, and not just mere extensions of the same old stereotypes. If all a writer or a filmmaker can do is give me the same crap that's always being presented, I'd rather just keep visiting these all White worlds, where people of color aren't seen, but at least they aren't humiliated. Although to be perfectly honest, neither option works for me.

Racism 2.0

"I wish I could say that racism and prejudice were only distant memories. We must dissent from the indifference. We must dissent from the apathy. We must dissent from the fear, the hatred and the mistrust." – Thurgood Marshall

After the election of Barack Obama in 2008, racism went away. The election of the first Black President of the United States magically transformed America into something known as "post-racial." It was truly spectacular to witness, as centuries of racial ideology went away, or reversed itself, or whatever it was that happened when American became post-racial, and this country was transformed into an idyllic nation of equality. Unfortunately, if you blinked, you would have missed this incredible turn of events, and in turn you would not have noticed a split second later, when America ceased being post-racial, and returned to its old racial ideologies with so much fury and speed that it seemed like racism may have gotten a bionic upgrade. Indeed, after America's brief flirtation with being post-racial, which again, lasted for all of one or two seconds, we all woke up to what I affectionately like to call "Racism 2.0."

The word racism, the concept it represents, the perceptions, assumptions, and implications associated with it, are at the center of the one of America's most challenging debates. Indeed, defining racism itself is problematic. Most people have a concept of what it is, though these concepts differ from person

131

to person, informed by things like racial identity, personal history, and education. In the end, the understanding of racism is for many people as the understanding of obscenity was for Supreme Court Justice Potter Stewart—"I know it when I see it." And because there are so many perceptions and understandings of what racism is or is not, and who is racist or who is not, the inability to define it makes it difficult to discuss or move beyond. If we as human beings are to move past the ideological constructs of racism, we must first come to grips with what it means. Racism is about more than hate, prejudice, oppression, or discrimination—it is about all of these, combined with power. Dr. Joy DeGruy explains:

> This then is racism. It is the belief that people differ along biological and genetic lines and that one's own group is superior to another group. This belief is coupled with the power to negatively effect the lives of those perceived to be inferior. (p. 23)

DeGruy is careful to point out that racism is belief paired with power. And by power, she does not mean physical strength. It is here—in the definition of power—that the definition of racism begins its perilous journey down the slippery slope of subjectivity and semantics. The reality of oppression on a racial level (as well as cultural, gender, and other levels) is that in order for a large number of people with shared attributes or commonalities to be oppressed, the oppressor must wield power beyond physical strength. Feagin defines power in its relation to racism as being "both the means of concrete oppression and the means of symbolizing and thinking about that domination" (p. 14). In other words, the power that is coupled with racism is the power to create a system of oppression, and then enforce that system upon a large number of people.

All too often I hear people say things like, "You know, Black people can be racists too," or "White people can be victims of racism too." Statements like these have led to many heated arguments—even amongst some of the most intelligent and informed people I have ever known. Unfortunately, anyone who thinks that White Americans as a group can be oppressed because of their race, or that Black people are capable of being racist, are completely wrong. Yes, White people in America can experience racial oppression, most often on an individual or small group level, but not as a population. I'm sorry, but a White kid who goes to a predominantly Black school, and gets picked on and beat up, is the victim of racist behavior, but not racism itself. The reason why is because despite the individual oppression this White kid may be feeling, he or she only feels its effects within a very limited set of circumstances, which can potentially be altered simply by changing environments. This is where we see the difference between being the victim of racist behavior, and being a victim of actual racism.

Anyone at any time can display racist behavior. In its most simple form, racist behavior is action, thought, or the combination of the two derived from the belief that someone is inferior based on their racial identification. To that end, Black people can indeed demonstrate racist behavior, either towards other races, or, sadly, towards other Black people. It is crucial, however, to understand that racist behavior is different from racism, because it lacks any power beyond the individual. Racist behavior says, "I don't like you because you look different, and so I will treat you differently." Racism says, "I don't like you because you look different, and

Barack Hussein Obama became the first person of color elected to the office of President of the United States. Many people thought his election meant that America had finally worked through its issues with race and racism. These people were idiots. Obama's election only proved that individual Blacks can be perceived differently, but as a group, African Americans still suffer from the same ideological constructs surrounding race that have made life in the United States unpleasant at times.

so I will treat you differently, and I have the power—politically, economically, and socially—to oppress a significant number of people who look just like you." This is what is called systemic racism, and it is the heart and soul of what ails America. Feagin elaborates:

> Systemic racism includes the complex array of antiblack practices, the unjustly gained political-economic power of whites, the continuing economic and other resource inequalities along racial lines, and the white racist ideologies and attitudes created to maintain and rationalize white privilege and power. Systemic here means that the core racist realities are manifested in each of society's major parts…[T]he economy, politics, education, religion, the family—reflects the fundamental reality of systemic racism. (p. 6)

The election of Barack Obama in 2008 signaled to some people an end to systemic racism. After all, how could America still be racist, if it elected the person of color to the highest position of power in the country? This line of questioning posits that the success of an individual of color—in this case a man of African descent—is the measure of the success, and by default, acceptance, of all people of color. This is the same line of thought applied by people who say that the Confederacy seceded from the Union over the right to own slaves, but the Civil War didn't actually have anything to do with slavery. In both cases, this type of thinking is reflective of an inability to look at racial identification through a realistic framework, because to do so would reveal very ugly truths.

To be honest, the emergence of Racism 2.0 in the wake of Obama's election didn't come as much of a surprise—at least not to Black people. We were all surprised by Obama's victory, and most of us felt that his election had in fact signaled the turning of some type of corner in terms of racial ideology. But only the most naïve or outright idiotic Black people thought racism had gone away. And of course, a lot of White people thought racism was gone. After all, that would have been convenient. It would have meant that one of the greatest evils committed in the formation of this country had suddenly been absolved and gone away, with no need for reconciliation or atonement. This would have been perfect for America, a nation plagued with obesity that is looking for a cure that does not involve eating well or exercising. That same mentality was applied to racism, which should have gone away with the election of Obama. Instead, it came back as Racism 2.0, which has proven to be like those cockroaches that survive being doused with the deadliest of bug sprays.

Since his election and re-election, there has been considerable debate over how Obama won. In the aftermath of the 2008 campaign, the reason was that American had become post-racial. This was quickly proven to be untrue, so when Obama was re-elected in 2012, despite Racism 2.0, attention was focused on how he ran his campaign. If there was any one general consensus, it was simply that Obama mounted a better campaign than his opponent, Mitt Romney—not necessarily that he was a better candidate, or even simply a better person. By examining Obama's "ground game"—how his campaign was run on the Internet and in the real world—the issue of race was not addressed, making it possible to avoid discussing the rise of Racism 2.0 in the wake of Obama's post-racial victory. What begins to emerge is a pattern of cognitive dissonance, at the heart of which is this adamant desire to not deal with the true issues of race and racism. First, Obama wins in 2008, and racism has magically gone away, so we don't need to talk about it anymore. Then, when racism comes back with a vengeance, we simply don't bother dealing with it during the 2012 campaign, and in the post-election coverage, campaign strategies are discussed so that as a nation we don't enter back into the discussion of how race factored into the election.

If left to our own devices, much of America would be more than happy to discuss race as it relates to Obama by simply saying, "He was the first Black president." Unfortunately, I'm not one of those people content with that version of history. I want to know how a Black man was elected President of the United States in 2008, when between 1882 and 1968, there were more than 3,000 recorded lynchings of Blacks throughout America, and anti-lynching legislation could not pass Congress for much of the twentieth century. I want to understand how a nation with legal and enforced racial segregation for most of its history, can progress enough to elect one of the oppressed into office. To put it in greater perspective, at the time of Barack Obama's birth to a White mother and a Black father in 1961, interracial relationships were against the law in seventeen states. Despite those that would call Obama bi-racial, multi-racial, half-White, or whatever terms that can be thought of to diminish his status as a Black man, there have been numerous laws of in this country set up to identify him as a Black man.

During slavery, as a means to delineate between the races, and thereby continue the justification of slavery based on race, there had to be a means of determining racial identification. From this was born the concept popularly referred to as the "one-drop rule." Different states had different methods of interpreting the one-drop rule, but its meaning was essentially the same: a person with any known African ancestors was to be considered Black. This means of determining race harkens back to the seventeenth century laws determining the status of the child based on the status of the mother. A child born to a slave mother was considered a slave, regardless of the status of the father. These laws allowed White slave owners to rape their female slaves, and then claim their offspring as property. The one-drop rule emerged as a way to identify Blacks, even though key racial characteristics may have become less prominent as a result of one parent being White. If it could be proven that a person had African ancestors, it made them Black in the eyes of the law. The one-drop rule became an effective tool in slavery, as well as the enforcement of segregation laws after the Emancipation Proclamation. F. James Davis points out, "Not only does the one-drop rule apply to no other group than American Blacks, but apparently the rule is unique in that it is found only in the United States and not in any other nation in the world" (p. 13).

The one-drop rule was more than a theory practiced from state to state. By the twentieth century, it was a law in many states. In 1924, Virginia passed the Racial Integrity Act, requiring the birth of every person born in the state to be recorded under one of two racial classifications, "White" or "Colored." Similar laws turned up in other states, and even with no laws on the books, the one-drop rule was used as a means of racial identification, even for people who showed no visible physical attributes of being Black. In fact, all it took in some places was the accusation of a Black ancestor, and a person's racial identification was set. It is important to understand this reality, if for no other reason to contrast it to how Obama has been presented by many people looking to identify him as something other than Black. By the laws once in place throughout this country, Obama is a Black man, despite the fact that his mother was White. The problem is that so many people either don't know about these laws, or have willfully forgotten, that conversations surrounding the one-drop rule and other forms of systemic racism are frequently left out of the debate over Obama's race. The result is an uneven dialog that seeks to take place within the sociopolitical framework of history, without knowing much about history. This is how America was able to become post-racial for a few seconds.

There are a variety of factors that led to the election of Barack Obama,

Jackie Robinson became an Exceptional Negro when he became the first Black player in Major League Baseball. Exceptional Negros are Black people who are perceived as being different from other African Americans. In reality, however, Exceptional Negros are just individuals who defy the accepted identifiers used to define race, which serve to dehumanize Blacks.

ranging from economic issues to the anti-Republican malaise that gripped the nation, as well as other factors that can be addressed outside the context of race. But when it comes to race, racism, or America becoming post-racial, the factors leading to Obama's election are not that difficult to trace, provided you are willing to look at ugly truths, ask difficult questions, and not back down from the legacy of race and racism in America. If we do this, we can trace the sociopolitical shift in racial perceptions, the reflection of these shifts in popular culture, and the emergence of a new class of racial identification that leads directly to the office of the President of the United States. The problem with doing this—for all you academic types looking for documented, empirical evidence—is that to the best of my knowledge it doesn't exist. What I am about to put forth is all theoretical, though some day, if America ever gets around to really dealing with race and racism, everyone will see that I'm correct.

The creation of a system of identification based on physical appearance (skin color), and the assertion that people physically identified as being Black were inferior to Whites, is the ideology upon which this nation was built. This racial ideology has been in place, in varying degrees, since the 1600s, and it has affected every facet of life in America, leading to the systemic oppression of a large number of Black people (as well as other people of color and women). From before the formation of this nation, when it was still a British colony, there have been challenges to the ideologies of race, though none of these challenges have succeeded in completely changing these ideological constructs. The failure of Reconstruction in the aftermath of the Civil War is one of the best examples of how things did not change. The failure of

Reconstruction, however, did not mean an end to the struggle for equality and justice for all, and that struggle continued in earnest, culminating most famously in the Civil Rights Movement of the mid-twentieth century.

From a sociopolitical standpoint, as well as an ideological one, the Civil Rights Movement represents the most sweeping changes in the experience of Black Americans since the abolition of slavery. Laws were enacted banning segregation, and with the move toward desegregation, there came a greater visibility for Blacks. Schools, neighborhoods, businesses, and workplaces that had been closed to African Americans in the past began to gradually open up, and as a result a new framework of inclusion emerged. This level of inclusion did not, however, bring equality, and in many parts of the nation the same old ideological beliefs of racial inferiority and superiority lingered, not only on personal levels, but on a systemic level. Still, there is no denying that starting with the end of World War II, up to the 1980s, there were some incredible changes in how Blacks—or at least some Blacks—were perceived. These changes were a direct result of political action, but it is the reflection of these political changes in the world of popular culture that seldom gets adequately addressed.

Up until the election of Barack Obama, the best measure of how the perception of Black people had changed in this country could be seen in the world of entertainment. This is not to say that the world of entertainment is more important than the political frontlines where the war of equality and ideology had been fought. On the contrary, this is merely to say that the perception of change is processed and packaged through a lens of popular culture and entertainment in a way that is more palatable to the average American. This is witnessed in the rise of popular Black athletes like Jackie Robinson, who broke baseball's color barrier, or singers like Nat King Cole and actors like Sidney Poitier who became major stars. Black athletes and entertainers emerged as ambassadors of race during the Civil Rights Movement, and through them, much of White America became accepting of Blacks. The important thing to keep in mind is that this acceptance was on a more individual level, and seldom extended to the Black population in general. It is within this context that what I like to call the "Exceptional Negro" began to emerge.

The concept of the Exceptional Negro has its roots in W.E.B. Du Bois's 1903 essay "The Talented Tenth," in which he writes, "The Negro race, like all races, is going to be saved by its exceptional men." Du Bois goes on the explain that "it is the problem of developing the Best of this race that they may guide the Mass away from the contamination and death of the Worst," placing the fate of Black Americans in the hands of what he calls the Talented Tenth—the best of the Black race. More than a century later, Black America is still waiting for the Talented Tenth, though a variation of this concept has emerged in the form of the Exceptional Negro, individual Blacks who find greater acceptance and success than the majority of other Blacks.

The world of sports, entertainment, and politics are filled with Exceptional Negroes, their success a testimony to "not being like other Blacks." Time and time again, that is how Exceptional Negroes like Oprah Winfrey, Michael Jordan, Denzel Washington, and Barack Obama are described—usually by White people. The concept of the Exceptional Negro, however, extends beyond the world of sports, entertainment, and politics, only on a much smaller scale. With the desegregation of America's school, neighborhoods, businesses, and workplaces,

142

Exceptional Negros began to appear all over the country. These were the individual Blacks who became known to White people on a more personal level, sometimes becoming close friends. Each one of these relationships potentially produced Exceptional Negroes who, to the White people that got know them, seemed to transcend race. This perception or racial transcendence is, in fact, a counteraction to the dehumanization produced through racial ideology. The dehumanization of Blacks has been so pervasive, however, that it is difficult for Whites (and some Blacks) to perceive Exceptional Negros as being Black. White people respond to the Exceptional Negro with the dubious compliment of, "You're not like other Blacks," while some Blacks respond to the Exceptional Negro by saying, "You're not really Black." In both cases, these statements are made because of the acceptance of ideological Black inferiority.

The Exceptional Negro provided select African Americans an opportunity to integrate a variety of fields, bringing with them a shift in racial perceptions that only applied to individuals that distinguished themselves as being different. These differences were marked by any number of positive attributes seldom attributed to Blacks—hard working, intelligent, creative, articulate, trustworthy, etc. It is important to note that with a handful of exceptions within the realm or politics and sociopolitical activism, the vast majority of high profile Exceptional Negros were in the world of entertainment. Through film, television, sports, and popular music, Black entertainers were transformed into   Exceptional Negros. This transformation was the direct result of the work of sociopolitical leaders and activists, but in the end the transformation seldom took place on a wide scale level. For every athlete who signs a multi-million dollar deal, or every Will Smith movie that becomes a blockbuster, there are still millions of Black people living in poverty, whose existence is controlled by systemic racism. And because of the long-term, multigenerational effects of racial ideology, it is easier to accept the dehumanization of most African Americans by simply saying that Michael Jordan and Denzel Washington are not like other Blacks, than it is to say, "Perhaps it is time we reconsider what we think of Black people, and why we think that way."

Although it would be dismissed by most historians and academics, it is possible to create a diagram of Exceptional Negroes in a variety of fields, all of whom are responsible in very specific ways to the election of Obama. Political

Trayvon Martin, an unarmed 17-year-old was gunned down by George Zimmerman on February 26, 2012. Although Zimmerman stood trial for the killing, it was Martin who was really on trial. The divide in public opinion surrounding the case revealed the striking disparity in how race is viewed in this nation.

figures like Martin Luther King Jr., Jesse Jackson, Medgar Evars, and Carl Stokes certainly belong on this diagram, and their contributions to Obama's election are obvious. But then there are people on the list like Bill Cosby, Tiger Woods, Oprah Winfrey, and Morgan Freeman, who have, in their own way, contributed to the acceptance of Exceptional Negros by White America, which in turn opened the door to the possibility of a politician like Obama. You could realistically draw a timeline from Jackie Robinson going to play for the Dodgers in the 1940s, to the birth of rock and roll in the 1950s (known then as "race music), to the blaxploitation films of the 1970s, to Bill Cosby's immensely popular television series of the 1980s, to Oprah Winfrey's rise as a media mogul of the 1990s, and have all these things lead directly to the Obama presidency.

What we have witnessed with the election of Barack Obama is the ascension of an Exceptional Negro to the office of the President of the United States. This is part of the reason why so many people have attempted to define Obama racially in various ways other than being Black. Quite simply, given the effective dehumanization of African Americans, the only way Obama can be the president is if he is either "not like other Blacks," or if he is "not really Black," both of which make him an Exceptional Negro. His election serves as a bittersweet example of how racial identification and perceptions have shifted over the last fifty years, proving that it is possible for ideological constructs to change for Blacks, but only on an individual level. As a people, we are still denied our humanity.

Perhaps more important than showing how racial ideology can shift to produce what appears to be exceptions to the accepted identifiers of Black people, Obama's election has helped to expose the depth of lingering ideological constructs. This again is what we call Racism 2.0. For some people, lulled into complacency by an age of political correctness, or who mistake the success of Exceptional Negros as a measure of success for all Blacks, Racism 2.0 may seem exceptionally virulent. Of course, it should be taken into consideration than in its initial incarnation, racism included the oppression of an entire population based on physical appearance, including enslavement for life, murder, rape, and the complete reduction of human life into that of property. By comparison to this earlier manifestation of racial oppression, Racism 2.0 simply isn't that bad. That said, it is still horrible and completely dehumanizing, feeding into systemic oppression that has dictated the course of countless millions of lives for more than four centuries.

The thing to keep in mind about Racism 2.0 is that it has a level of visibility that makes it more obvious. This visibility is in part the result of Obama's election, and the perception of Blacks rising up from their place of inferiority to usurp power from the superior White race. Racism 2.0 is more visible and more vocal because with the growing numbers of Exceptional Negros there is an increased desperation to hold on to the ideologies that define racism itself. But it is important to keep in mind that these ideologies have never gone away. Nor did Obama resurrect these ideologies, as if he were some voodoo witch doctor, inadvertently bringing racist zombies back to life by repeatedly chanting, "Yes we can." Racism has always run rampant in America, allowing for the enslavement of Africans and the genocide of Native Americans. And no matter what changes may have occurred within the sociopolitical realm, none of it brought an end to the notions of White superiority. That simply did not happen.

What did happen is that the older version of racism learned to hide, making itself less visible to the public. At some point it became the house next door, where the neighbors keep the windows closed and the shades drawn, making it difficult to see what is going on inside. But after the election of Obama, the shades were raised and the windows opened, allowing everyone to see what was going on inside the house. What's more, the door of this house was left open as well, and out wandered Racism 2.0, like a neighbor you haven't actually seen in years, who proceeds to dance around the front yard naked, without a care in the world. Racism 2.0 acts as if dancing around the front yard, completely naked, is normal and acceptable—as if no one else will notice what it is doing, or how it appears. And this mentality has manifested itself everywhere from the horrifically racist statements that litter the comment sections on countless websites, to the pro-hate messages of political leaders who seem oblivious to what they've just said. In fact, if Racism 2.0 has a motto, it would be, "hatred, unashamed and unaware."

Perhaps the most insidious aspect of Racism 2.0—aside from the way it prances around, blissfully unaware of its own existence—is the culture of denial that enables and nurtures it. This is the same culture of denial that allowed slavery to thrive, the Lost Cause narrative of the Civil War to be accepted as reality and, now, Racism 2.0 to flourish amidst the misguided belief that America has become post racial. Racism and racists have always thrived in a climate of denial and rationalization, which seeks to explain away deeds of oppression, marginalization, and victimization by placing the burden of proof on the victim. This is the heart and soul of Racism 2.0—the lifeblood that allows it to endure when so many people claim it no longer exists. Put quite simply, the greatest weapon of a racist society is the ability to say to those who have fallen victim to acts of racism, "Prove it."

Proving the existence and effects of racial ideologies of inferiority and superiority seems like it would be easy enough, but then we must stop and consider that as a society, America can't even come to an agreement on what is and is not racist. The inability to agree on what is and is not racist has become increasingly clear following the election of President Obama, the increasing number of Exceptional Negroes, and, of course, the brief moment of being post racial that many of us missed because we blinked our eyes. With startling regularity, this country faces moments of racism and the effects of lingering racial ideology that are being met with a refusal of acceptance and responsibility that can only be mustered by people who exist at the top of the ideological pyramid (or those vying for a place at the top). From the newly coded terminology used by Obama's critics to call him a nigger without actually calling him a nigger, to the supporters of a killer like George Zimmerman, there has been an increase in the denial of racism, as well as the need of the victim to prove they have been attacked.

In a society that claims to protect the victim, those on the receiving end of racism provide a glimpse at the flagrant hypocrisy that provides the tune so many Americans blissfully sing along with. When it comes to the oppression and victimization of others based on race—not to mention gender—there is almost no protection of the victim. Black people have seen this time and time again, we try to talk about it—some even scream and yell and jump around—only to be told that what we are experiencing is not racism, or that we're being "too sensitive," or we are playing the "race card," or "get over it," or "go back to Africa." All of these reactions are part of the multigenerational, systemic dehumanization of people of color in the United States, which not only seeks to rob us of our humanity, but also admonishes us for trying to assert ourselves as human beings.

Black people in America must never lose sight of one simple fact—as a group we are not human beings. Individually, some of us have been given our humanity, but it is only granted on a moment-to-moment basis. People of African descent were stripped of their humanity as a means to justify slavery, and even though slavery has been abolished—or at least partially abolished (because the current prison system suggests something to the contrary)—humanity has not been something restored to people of color. Racial ideologies in this country created a system of racial inferiority and superiority, in which blacks were dehumanized and made to be inferior. It is this dehumanization and the ideology that nurtures it that allowed an unarmed seventeen-year-old like Trayvon Martin to be gunned down by someone like George Zimmerman, and to have his killer be found not guilty on all charges. And the reason Zimmerman got away with killing Martin has far less to do with the legal technicalities of the state of Florida, and more to do with the long-standing ideological constructs that denies Martin his status as a human being.

The case of Trayvon Martin is just one of many that involve the killing of a Black American in an act fueled by racial ideology, and then a raging debate over whether or not racism was involved. Ideological lines were drawn in the Martin case, with both sides contesting the role of race and racism in the tragic events that occurred, and in the middle lay the dead body of a teenage boy. To make matters worse, the subsequent trial of his killer, George Zimmerman, was not to determine the guilt or innocence of the shooter, but of the victim. Make no mistake, Zimmerman's trial was in fact Martin's trial, and as such, it stands as a glaring example of how the ideological constructs of race actually work.

America prides itself on the concept of "innocent until proven guilty," which sounds really good, along with phrases like "all men are created equal," and all that stuff about inalienable rights provided by the Constitution. But the fact of the matter is that presumed innocence is not explicitly provided by the Constitution and in studying the origins of the supreme law of the United States, it is clear that it was not drafted with all the citizens of America in mind. Joe Feagin explains, "At the heart of the Constitution was the protection of the property and wealth of the affluent bourgeoisie in the new nation, including property in those enslaved" (p. 2).

The point that must be understood is that not only does the Constitution of the United States not explicitly provide for the presumption of innocence, it was not originally drafted to protect people who at the time had no rights. This combination of factors played out for all the world to see during the Trayvon Martin case, in which the presumption of innocence brought with it the presumption that someone must be guilty— and therein lies a paradoxical flaw of the criminal justice system. If the accused, Zimmerman, was to be presumed innocent, then someone must have been guilty. When all was said and done, it was Trayvon Martin who was on trial. In finding Zimmerman innocent, Martin was found guilty. Never mind the fact that Martin was the victim. Think about it. The only way Zimmerman could be innocent was if Martin was guilty of something that justified his being killed. An armed adult killed an unarmed teenager, and a jury decided it was the victim's fault.

This is where the real problem in America starts to come into the light. The same ideological constructs that favors White men in this country, also serves to bestow upon them the presumption of innocence. But with that great gift, someone must always face the presumption of guilt. How many women have suffered sexual assaults, only to face allegations that they somehow did something wrong or provoked their attack? How many Blacks have been brutalized and murdered, because they acted inappropriately around White people? Those that can be counted amongst the oppressed—by virtue of race, gender, or sexual identity—know all too well that when we accuse someone of oppressing us, the burden of proof is on us. Women must prove that they are the victims of sexual harassment and sexual assault. People of color must prove that they are the victims of racial discrimination. A system that places burden of proof on the victim is a broken system built on oppression and ideological constructs, with clearly defined roles of who is inferior and who is superior.

The sad fact of the matter is that racism is the very foundation upon which this nation was built. People of color were stripped of their humanity and presented as being inferior, to justify acts of brutality that were committed for centuries. Feagin writes, "Indeed, in the first two centuries of the new nation the majority of White Americans, in spite of the professed ethic of liberty, saw nothing wrong with the brutal subordination of Black Americas or the driving away or killing of Native Americans" (p. 14). And it was not just Blacks or Native Americas who were framed within a context of inferiority and systemically oppressed. The same thing happened to women. A close examination of American history reveals that the founding fathers never intended to share life, liberty, or the pursuit of happiness with anyone other than their fellow White, property-owning men of means.

The more you study the history of this country, the more certain truths are revealed. In time, it becomes clear that as a nation we have all been infected by ideologies of racial inferiority and superiority. To put it another way, racism is a disease, and every single American, no matter what their background, has been affected and infected by this insidious disease. Patterns of racial identification, and the ideological constructs upon which these patterns have been built, are interwoven into the day-to-day experiences, perceptions, and interactions of all Americans. Some of the effects of racism are obvious and easy to spot, and others are so innocuous and interwoven in the fabric of this nation that they simply appear to be "normal." Whichever the case, we still live in a society of the oppressed and the oppressors. On a daily basis, we must live with this oppression, as we go about or lives—some of us living under the perception that we are inferior, simply by virtue of the beliefs and perceptions tied to our physical appearance. We struggle day by day to regain the humanity that was taken from us. Meanwhile, our oppressors, who may or may not be aware of their culpability in the long-enduring game of race and racial identification, do not emerge unharmed from these circumstances. It is impossible for White people to dehumanize people of color the way they have for so long—either intentionally or unintentionally—without giving away a huge part of their humanity. Paulo Freire (1970) explains, "Dehumanization, which marks not only those whose humanity has been stolen, but also (though in a different way) those who have stolen it, is a distortion of the vocation of becoming more fully human" (p. 44).

In the end, as we look at the concept of race in this country—a concept that has sadly spread across the globe—we see that America is a nation that has traded its humanity for personal and economic gain. People of color were robbed of their humanity to justify these gains, while White people traded their humanity to make these gains. This is what happened during slavery, and it continues today wherever people are being oppressed, exploited and, in some cases, killed for the sake of riches. And no matter where any of us lands on the racial spectrum, we all must come to terms with our culpability in this on-going process of weighing human life against the accumulation of wealth. It has left us diseased and broken, and the collective unwillingness to look at what has happened to us brings with it nothing more than the promise of our continued dehumanization.

Evolutionary Being

"Blinding ignorance does mislead us. O! Wretched mortals, open your eyes!" – Leonard da Vinci

For Americans, the act of dehumanizing others comes a bit too easily. We are, after all, a nation built upon systemic, multigenerational dehumanization. Perhaps it would be easier to repair the damage that has been done—to take this country in a new direction of equality and justice—if it were merely a question of liberating the oppressed from their oppressors. But it is not that simple, for even within the ranks of the oppressed you can find oppressors, clinging tight to ideological beliefs of inferiority and superiority that place them above someone else. The act of dehumanization is so ingrained in us as a culture, that it is second nature to many people, trumping religion and politics as the defining factor of who a person is and how they think. It is a sad truth for many Americans, but finding reasons to hate others has become the only way some people can feel better about themselves. We are a nation of people who seek to prove their strength by attacking those we have deemed weak.

Despite my light complexion and my manner of speech, I was identified as being Black, and grew up under the identifiers associated with that distinction. I was a member of the Black community, and as such, I was the member of a community that had been systemically oppressed for centuries. I often felt this oppression in a variety of ways that are too long to list and too painful to forget. And yet, as a member of this community of the oppressed, I—like many others within this same community—did my fair share of oppressing. When I look into my personal rearview mirror, I see my past prejudices down the road I've travelled. There's no mistaking the wreckage caused by my sexism, or my homophobia, or any of the other injustices and dehumanization I engaged in simply because I longed to feel better about myself. Sadly, the same is true not for some of us, but for all of us. Whether conscious or unconscious, we have all hurt others to heal our own pain.

I take no pride in admitting that I have prejudices. It pains me to admit to the homophobia I once felt. I take no comfort that I am more mindful of sexism and gender discrimination than I once was, because I still fall into the trap of engaging in both, despite my desires to the contrary. If I am to be perfectly honest, part of me would just as soon forget all my acts of oppression and dehumanization, but that would do me no good. If I were able to erase all the things I've done wrong, I would be erasing the lessons learned, leaving myself in the horrific position of reliving the same events over and over again. Day in and day out, I would be seeking to regain my own humanity at the expense of others—robbing them of their rights and dignity because mine seemed to have been taken from me. So many of us have done this. So many of us continue to do this. And it is this act of erasing history—of altering what has happened in an effort to ease the soul—that has created the world we live in.

All of this leads us to a single burning question: How do we restore our individual humanity without depriving others their humanity?

I have pondered this question, and the questions that come along with it, because to be clear, one question will always lead to another. But for the moment—in the here and now of what I'm trying to share with anyone willing to pay attention—there is just this question. *How do we restore our individual humanity without depriving others their humanity?*

It seems to me that each of us must first recognize our individual humanity. My humanity is mine, just as yours belongs to you. Others may seek to rob us of it, but it belongs to us. And more important, humanity cannot be truly taken. It can be damaged—perhaps even broken—and it can be given away, but when push comes to shove, humanity can't be taken. Centuries of slavery and the racial ideology that emerged to justify slavery sought specifically to take humanity from millions of people, and yet they held on. My ancestors—the people whose blood flows through my veins—were bound and shackled for life. Families were torn apart. My great-great grandfather Nelson went to his grave never knowing what happened to his mother, who had been sold off to another plantation when he was a child. And yet Nelson held on to his humanity. He taught his children how to hold on to their humanity, who in turn taught their children. Make no mistake, this is no easy task, and some people—even some within my own family—never quite managed to hold on to their humanity. They got lost in the blinding storm of dehumanization that can surround us on a daily basis, and rather than fighting to assert themselves, they acquiesced to a myriad of abuses—both outward and inward—that leave so many damaged.

When we think of the endless ways we become damaged or the ways in which we can damage others, we are ultimately talking about dehumanization. It doesn't matter if it is slavery, substance abuse, or failing to offer a positive word to someone in need, it all stems from a disconnect with our own humanity. This disconnect acts like a disease.

The first step in fighting this disease is to find yourself—not the idea of who or what you are based on the perceptions or ideologies of the outside world—but who you are at your very core. This is perhaps the most difficult thing any of us will ever do. Bookshelves are littered with self-help guides designed to help us find success, overcome what obstacles we may face, and become overall better people. Churches, mosques, and synagogues are filled with people looking for something, and more often than not, that something is a way to reconnect with their humanity.

Several years ago I came across a quote from Pierre Teilhard de Chardin that struck me as being one of the most profound things I had read. At the time, I was unemployed, had just ended a relationship, was sliding down the slippery slope of depression, and felt like there was no hope. I won't go so far as to say it was the darkest time of my life, but it was pretty damn dark. And then I read this quote by de Chardin:

> ...I took the lamp and, leaving the zone of everyday
> occupations and relationships where everything seems
> clear, I went down into my innermost self, to the deep

abyss whence I feel dimly that my power of action emanates. But as I moved further and further away from the conventional certainties by which social life is superficially illuminated, I became aware that I was loosing contact with myself. At each step of the descent a new person was disclosed within me of whose name I was no longer sure, and who no longer obeyed me. And when I had to stop my exploration because the path had faded from beneath my steps, I found a bottomless abyss at my feet, and out of it came—arising I know not from where—the current which I dare to call my life. (p. 76)

At the time, the only thing I knew about de Chardin were these 139 words. I didn't know the larger context from which the quote was taken, but I did know that something about it stuck with me. I saved the quote, reading it over and over again, internalizing what it meant to me as I began to venture into the abyss from which my power of action emanates. Years later, I would read the book from which the quote was taken, de Chardin's *The Divine Milieu.* Initially, it was a difficult read. De Chardin was a Jesuit priest, and God and Christianity factored into *The Divine Milieu* so much that my own personal bias began to block not my understanding, but my willingness to look beyond the surface of what was being said. It was not until I let go of my own prejudice toward organized religion—and the connotations of what God and Christianity mean to me—that I began to understand that just because de Chardin's message was peppered with certain words, the message itself was greater than the words used to convey it. I began to think of it like this: de Chardin was a teacher and I was a student. I could become hung up on the words he used in his lesson, or I could look for the greater meaning of the lesson that comes from somewhere beyond words.

At some point, we must all venture into the abyss from which the power of action emanates. This power of action is the source of our humanity. De Chardin calls this source God. I don't have a term for it, nor do I seek to explain where the source comes from. I merely believe that it is there, no questions asked. It is who we are at our core—it is the potential for greatness that we all possess, despite the abuses that seek to say otherwise. But it is hidden so deep inside all of us, buried underneath a lifetime of pain and fear and humiliation and oppression, that to search for it means to dig through all that covers it. And for some people, looking for this true source of power is too much—they can't handle sifting through the crushing debris that buries their power, and so they just give up. They forego their humanity in favor of something that resembles survival, when in fact it is merely death in measured doses. There is no easy way to search for the power of action that dwells in the deepest, darkest region of your being, just as there is no easy way to examine the circumstances that seek to deny you that power, thereby threatening your very humanity. De Chardin writes:

> In the divine milieu all the elements of the universe touch each other by that which is most inward and ultimate in them. There they concentrate, little by little, all that is purest and most attractive in them without loss and without danger of subsequent corruption. There they shed, in their meeting, the mutual externality and the incoherences which form the basic pain of human relationships. Let those seek refuge

there who are saddened by the separations, the meannesses and the wastefulnesses of the world. In the external spheres of the world, man is always torn by the separations which set distance between bodies, which set the impossibility of mutual understanding between souls, which set death between lives. Moreover at every minute he must lament that he cannot pursue and embrace everything within the compass of a few years. Finally, and not without reason, he is incessantly distressed by the crazy indifference and the heart-breaking dumbness of a natural environment in which the greater part of the individual endeavor seems wasted or lost, where the blow and the cry seem stifled on the spot, without awakening an echo. (p. 114)

I wish I could tell you there is an easy way to understand systems of oppression and study such things as the issues of race and racism. Unfortunately, there is no comfortable way to deal with the realities of history, and the wholesale dehumanization that occurred under the rationalizations provided by racial ideology. And the same is true for all other constructs of oppression, marginalization, and injustice. To think about these things is to invite frustration, sorrow, anger, and depression into your home, where they will stay, as unwanted guests, leaching off the light of your soul. But the thing to keep in mind is that it is your own personal light that will fend off these unwanted guests. Others may try to take your humanity as if it is theirs to take—as if it is a precious commodity that can be bought or sold, stolen or given as a gift—and that is simply not the case. Your individual humanity is in fact a precious resource, and it can and will most definitely be impacted by all sorts of factors, but it does not belong to anyone else.

Ultimately, I believe that humanity—that is to say actually being human—is a state to which we must all evolve. A crucial part of this evolutionary process, of growing into your own humanity and thereby becoming the best human being we can possibly be, is to recognize that what is in you is in everyone else. We are all at various stages of our development, and the only way to attain any true level of humanity requires a combination of not denying that development to others, as well as helping others in their own growth. If you look around, there are plenty of terms to describe this process of evolving into our own humanity. De Chardin calls it establishing ourselves within the divine milieu. I call it "Evolutionary Being."

Evolutionary Being is to be in a constant state of growth and transformation. It is recognizing that who you are, is who you are becoming, and who you are becoming is who you are, and that neither is static. It is the answer to the question, and the question to the answer. It is the pursuit of knowledge and the sharing of knowledge, and it is understanding that one of our greatest fears is what we don't know. Perhaps the most common manifestation of this fear surrounds the uncertainty of death. We don't know for sure what happens after we die and it terrifies us—we are, after all, afraid of what we don't know. The fear of the unknown, however, extends far beyond death. Quite simply, we are all afraid of our own lack of knowledge on pretty much every level imaginable. And the fear we have for our own lack of knowledge transforms into intolerance when it comes to what we perceive as a lack of knowledge in others and ourselves. The fear of a lack of knowledge becomes a hatred for ignorance that we both externalize and internalize. We all do this. I do this. But it is not conducive to Evolutionary Being.

I can't speak for anyone else. I can't tell anyone else how to live, think, or even exist. But I can tell you what I do—how I work towards Evolutionary Being. This is what I tell myself on a daily basis, and the way I work to live my life.

I must stop fearing and hating a lack of knowledge—both in myself and others—and discard it as the first step toward Evolutionary Being. I must replace the fear and hatred of a lack of knowledge with a deeply personal love of the acquisition of knowledge. I must fall in love with learning—even if the things I am learning make me uncomfortable, reveal painful truths, or initially elude me. There are always lessons to be learned, and as I begin to acquire new knowledge, I cannot be afraid to let it change how I think. I cannot change other people, or deny anyone else the right to be who they are, even when I do not agree with them. The only thing I can do is inspire and influence others through the changes I am willing to make within myself. Change is transformation, transformation is evolution, and Evolutionary Being is always my goal.

Bibliography

Allen, R. (2001). *The Concept of Self: A Study of Black Identity and Self Esteem.*
Detroit, MI: Wayne State University Press.

Berry, S. T., Berry, V. (2001). *The 50 Most Influential Black Films.* New York,
NY: Citadel Press.

Bogle, D. (1994). *Toms, Coons, Mulatoes, Mammies & Bucks* (3rd ed.). New York,
NY: Continuum.

Boyd, T. (2007). *The Super Fly '70s.* New York, NY: Harlem Moon.

Burns, K. (1990). *The Civil War* [DVD]. United States: PBS

Burrell, T. (2010). *Brainwashed: Challenging the Myth of Black Inferiority.* New
York, NY: Smiley Books.

Campbell, J., Moyers, B. (1988). *The Power of Myth.* New York, NY:
Doubleday.

Cha-Jua, S.K. (2008). Black Audiences, Blaxploitation, and Kung Fu Films. In
P. Fu (Ed.), *China Forever: The Shaw Brothers and Diasporic Cinema.*
Chicago, IL: University of Illinois Press.

Chadwick, B. (2001). *The Reel Civil War: Mythmaking in American Film.* New
York, NY: Vintage Books

Charters, A. (1970). *Nobody: The story of Bert Williams.* New York, NY: Macmillan
Company.

Coombs, N. (1972). *The Black Experience in America: The Immigrant Heritage
of America.* (Electronic edition). Lisle, IL: Project Guttenberg.

Cripps, T. (1993). *Slow Fade to Black: The Negro in American Film, 1900-1942.*
New York, NY: Oxford University Press.

Cripps, T. (1993). *Making Movies Black: The Hollywood Message Movie from
World War II to the Civil Rights Era.* New York, NY: Oxford University Press.

Diawara, M. (1993). *Black American Cinema*. New York, NY: Routledge.

Dates, J., & Barlow, W. (Eds.). (1990). *Split Image: African Americans in the Mass Media*. Washington, D.C.: Howard University Press.

Davis, F. (1991). *Who is Black?*. University Park, Pennsylvania: The Pennsylvania State University Press.

De Chardin, P. T. (1960). *The Divine Milieu: An Essay on the Interior of Life*. New York, NY: Harper Torchbooks

DeGruy, J. (2005). *Post Traumatic Slave Syndrome: America's Legacy of Enduring Injury and Healing*. Portland, OR: Joy DeGruy Publications.

DuBois, W.E.B. (1989). *The Soul of Black Folks*. New York, NY: Penguin Books.

Ellison, R. (1952). Invisible Man. New York: Random House

Feagin, J.R. (2010). *Racist America: Roots, Current Realities and Future Reparations* (2nd ed.). New York, NY: Routledge.

Foner, E. (2005). *Forever Free: The Story of Emancipation and Reconstruction*. New York, NY: Alfred A. Knopf.

Ferrante, T. (1989, February). A Farewell to Duane Jones. *Fangoria* (80), 14-18.

Foner, E. (2005). *Forever Free: The Story of Emancipation and Reconstruction*. New York, NY: Alfred A. Knopf.

Freire, P. (1970). *Pedagogy of the Oppressed*. New York, NY: Continuum.

George, N. (1992). *Buppies, B-boys, Baps & Bohos*. New York, New York: Harper Collins.

George, N. (1994). *Blackface*, New York, NY: Harper Collins.

Grossberg, L., Wartella, E., Whitney, D.C., Wise, J.M. (2005). *MediaMaking: Mass Media in a Popular Culture*. Thousand Oaks, CA: Sage Publications.

Guerrero, E. (1993) *Framing Blackness: The African American Image in Film*. Philadelphia, PA: Temple University Press.

Hansen, J. (2000). *Bury Me Not in the Land of Slaves: African Americans in the Time of Reconstruction*. New York, NY: Grolier Publishing.

Horton, J., Horton, L. (2003). *Slavery and the Making of America*. New York, NY: Oxford University Press.

Kato, M.T. (2007). *From Kung Fu to Hip Hop: Globalization, Revolution, and Popular Culture.* Albany, NY: State University of New York.

Kolker, R. (2005). *Film, Form and Culture.* Columbus, OH: McGraw Hill.

Martinez, G., Martinez, D. & Chavez, A. (1998). *What It Is...What It Was!.* New York, NY: Hyperion

McGilligan, P. (2007). *Oscar Micheaux: The Great and Only.* New York, NY: Harper Perennial.

Middleton, R. (2007). The Historical Legal Construction of Black Racial Identity of Mixed Black-White Race Individuals: The Role of State Legislatures. *Jackson State University Researcher*, 21(2), 17-39.

Parrillo, V. (2009). *Strangers to These Shores* (9th edition). Boston, MA: Pearson Education, Inc.

Penrice, R. (2007). *African American History for Dummies.* Hoboken, NJ: Wiley Publishing.

Poussaint, A.F. (1968). The Negro American: His Self-Image and Integration. In F.B. Barbour (Ed.). *The Black Power Revolt.* Boston, MA: Expanding Horizons Books.

Pryor, R. (1978). *Wanted: Richard Pryor Live in Concert.* [CD]. United States: Warner Bros. Records.

Rausch, A.J. (2011). *I Am Hip-Hop: Conversations on the Music and the Culture.* Lanham, MD: Scarecrow Press.

Reid, M. (1993). *Redefining Black Film.* Berkley, CA: University of California Press.

Richards, L. (1998). *African American Films Through 1959.* Jefferson, NC: McFarland & Company, Inc.

Roediger, D.R. (2008). *How Race Survived U.S. History: From Settlement to Slavery to the Obama Phenomenon.* New York, NY: Verso.

Stewart, J. (2005). *Migrating to the Movies: Cinema and Black Urban Modernity.* Berkley, CA: University of California Press.

Walker, D., Rausch, A. & Watson, C. (2009) *Reflections on Blaxploitation.* Lanham, MD: The Scarecrow Press.

Watkins, M. (1994). *On the Real Side: A History of African American Comedy.*
Chicago, IL: Lawrence Hill Books.

Van Ausdale, D., Feagin, J. R. (2001). *The First R: How Children Learn Race and Racism.* Lanham, MD: Rowman & Littlefield.

Zinn, H. (1995). *A People's History of the United States 1492-Present.* New York, NY: Harper Collins

About the Author

David F. Walker is an award-winning writer, filmmaker, and pop culture critic. He is best known for being the creator of the pop culture 'zine *BadAzz MoFo,* and the author of the Young Adult series *The Adventures of Darius Logan.* He has also written comic books, including the *Number 13* for Dark Horse Comics, and *The Army of Dr Moreau* for Monkeybrain Comics. In addition to writing, he has made several films, including the award-winning short *Black Santa's Revenge.* When not writing, David is usually doing laundry. He is a Sagittarius and lives in Portland, Oregon.